NATIVE AMERICAN RESISTANCE

Resource Book

ABC-CLIO

National History
Day, Inc.

PROJECT EDITOR
Holly Leck, *Manager, Resource Book Development*

EDITORIAL
Padraic Carlin, *Manager, Editorial Development*
Andrew McCormick, *Writer/Editor*
Maxine Taylor, *Writer/Editor*

MEDIA ACQUISITIONS
Caroline Price, *Manager, Media Resources*

PRODUCTION
Vicki Moran, *Senior Production Editor*
Don Schmidt, *Manager, Books Production*
Paula Gerard, *File Management Coordinator*

Ann Claunch, *Director of Curriculum*

Library of Congress Cataloging-in-Publication Data
Native American resistance : resource book / [project editor Holly Leck].
    p. cm. — (The individual in history)
  "National History Day."
  Includes bibliographical references.
  ISBN 978-1-59884-183-1
  1. Indians of North America—Government relations—Study and teaching—Activity programs.
2. Indians of North America—Politics and government—Study and teaching—Activity programs.
3. United States—Ethnic relations—Study and teaching—Activity programs.   4. United States—
Politics and government—Study and teaching—Activity programs.   I. Leck, Holly.
E93.N2858 2008
323.1197—dc22

                                                                2008012663

COVER PHOTO: Gilbert Blue Bird rides past the Wounded Knee Massacre Site on Thursday, June 1, 2006 outside of Wounded Knee, South Dakota in the Pine Ridge Reservation. (NewSport/Corbis)

Contents

About the Development Team

DR. JOHN P. BOWES
EASTERN KENTUCKY UNIVERSITY

John P. Bowes is an assistant professor of history at Eastern Kentucky University where he teaches classes on Native American history and U.S. history. He received his bachelor's degree from Yale University and his doctorate from the University of California at Los Angeles. John is the author of three books that examine Indian removal in the 19th century. One of those, *Exiles and Pioneers: Eastern Indians in the Trans-Mississippi West*, focuses on the removal and postremoval experience of four Indian communities from the Great Lakes region.

CHRIS MULLIN
SANTA YNEZ VALLEY UNION HIGH SCHOOL

Chris Mullin graduated from the University of California at Berkeley with a degree in classical Greek and Latin and received a master's degree in education from the University of California at Santa Barbara. Chris teaches Latin, Advanced Placement European history, and Advanced Placement U.S. history in the beautiful Santa Ynez Valley, California, at Santa Ynez Valley Union High School. Chris has been a fellow of the Teachers Network Leadership Institute and a facilitator for the California History-Social Science Project; he has developed numerous history-related classroom activities that he has presented at state and national conferences. In 2003, he was named California Teacher of the Year for his passionate and innovative approaches to teaching history. Chris is dedicated to finding innovative ways to introduce primary source materials into the day-to-day teaching of history. He believes in challenging students and encouraging them to see history not as a series of verifiable facts but as a compendium of open-ended questions. In lectures, he makes a point of revealing his own reflective process to help students hone their own critical thinking skills.

BRETT PIERSMA
SANTA YNEZ VALLEY UNION HIGH SCHOOL

Brett Piersma received his bachelor's degree in history and his master's degree in education and teaching credential at the University of California at Santa Barbara (UCSB). He teaches Advanced Placement European history, Advanced Placement American government, and college preparatory world cultures at Santa Ynez Valley Union High School in Santa Ynez, California. He has facilitated the California History-Social Sciences Project at UCSB and is a MetLife Fellow for the Teachers Network Leadership Institute. Brett has also cowritten several award-winning classroom activities. His many passions in teaching include designing primary source–based lesson plans, increasing teacher voice and leadership in schools, increasing student access to rigorous curricula, and perfecting the use of technology in the classroom. Among his innovative techniques are dress-up nights for Advanced Placement European history students that recreate an Enlightenment-era salon, complete with period music and debates on the works of Voltaire and Rousseau.

Foreword

The *Individual in History* series explores three social movements: the environmental movement, Native American resistance, and uncivil disobedience. The premise of the books illuminates a fundamental tenet of American democracy: individual citizens working toward the common good. Each resource book presents compelling stories of individuals with deep convictions and a belief that their actions would result in a better world, and highlights pivotal defining moments that illustrate both the brightest periods in our history and its darkest episodes. *Uncivil Disobedience* illustrates the myriad of choices people encounter in speaking out against an issue. What avenue is the most effective way to shift attitudes or change policies in society? Through violent action or passive resistance? How far is too far and how far is not far enough? *Native American Resistance* reveals the importance of the individual and leadership in a historical context. Under what conditions do leaders emerge? What are the attributes of a leader in a time of crisis? *Environmental Movement* demonstrates how individuals have challenged the general public to see into our future, to set aside immediate economic gain, and to think about the long-term impact on the quality of our lives. How will the individual influence widespread policy not only for immediate change but also as a legacy for future generations?

These questions continue to be debated and answered by the time and place in history in which the issues are confronted and the type of people who become the "voice of change." In *The Individual in History* series, the social movements of Native American resistance, uncivil disobedience, and the environmental movement will be examined through the issues challenged, the individuals who participated in the cause, and the legacy of their actions.

At their center, these resource books are devoted to providing each student with the raw materials to evaluate each issue on his or her own. In each workbook, students will find a wide array of primary materials: laws, poems, quotations, cartoons, speeches, editorials, and images. To help students interpret these historical documents and give them a solid grounding in the topic, secondary essays, glossaries, and background material are provided as well. This material, too, has been drawn from a great variety of sources: experts in diverse fields including education, political science, history, and literature.

Together, these primary and secondary sources form the building blocks for sets of classroom activities. These activities are designed to encourage students to analyze primary documents and to use their conclusions to evaluate the ways uncivil disobedience, Native American resistance, and the environmental movement have been handled throughout past centuries. Students are asked to debate, to role play, and to write creatively about the historical materials. At the conclusion of each activity, the students are asked to judge the actions of the parties involved and to unravel the complexities within each issue.

Each resource book features a series of essays designed to introduce students to each topic. The first essay is a broad issue overview. The second essay is more specific and chronological. Next, the workbooks present two defining moments—landmark historical events that illustrate the nature of debate on each topic. Each Defining Moment section begins with detailed background information. Next, classroom activities are provided, along with instructions and a list of materials needed to complete them. These materials, primary sources, and reference pieces follow each classroom activity section. The activities are broken down into parts, each one designed to challenge the students' assumptions and lead them to different conclusions. The last portion of the activity asks students to assess both the defining moment and the issue at large.

In partnering to compile *The Individual in History* series of resource books, ABC-CLIO and National History Day, Inc. continue their commitment to challenging students with historical material that both celebrates and complicates our concept of the national heritage. By combining quality research with active learning, we hope to bring the excitement of lively history and participatory civics to your classroom.

BECKY SNYDER
PRESIDENT, SCHOOLS PUBLISHER
ABC-CLIO

CATHY GORN
EXECUTIVE DIRECTOR
National History Day, Inc.

Using This Resource Book

The Individual in History resource books are designed to provide teachers with all the materials to create interactive lessons centered on a single important topic of American history. In each lesson, students are asked to analyze primary historical documents and draw conclusions about the topic. You will find two sets of suggested classroom activities in each book. For each activity, we have provided background essays, source documents, and reference pieces.

THE MATERIALS ARE ORGANIZED AS FOLLOWS:

1. INTRODUCTION

The essay in this section is a broad overview of the resource book's topic. You may use it to create a general lesson or lecture on the issue at hand, or to prepare students for the historical analysis portions.

2. THROUGHOUT HISTORY

The material provided here is geared to specific subtopics within the broader issue—for example, evolving strategies of environmentalists or civil disobedience approaches of various individuals. This material may be used to create a preparatory lecture for the resource book's interactive portions or copied and handed out for students to read.

3. DEFINING MOMENTS I AND II

Each resource book features two defining moments, or spotlights on significant events in history that illustrate key issues related to the overall theme of the book. Each defining moment contains an introduction, a series of classroom activities, primary and secondary sources, and background material. Following is a description of each of these four sections.

a. Introduction

A key historical event is presented to illustrate the problems and complex forces at work within each topic. The Defining Moment section begins with a short historical background essay that provides context for the classroom activities. Again, this piece may be used to organize a short presentation or given to students to read before they begin the activities.

b. Classroom Activities

Each Defining Moment section includes a series of Classroom Activities, which are broken down into lessons, and the materials required for each lesson are noted. When the lesson calls for Activity Sheets, these are located with the Activity description. In some cases, portions of the Activity may stand alone, but they are designed to be cumulative. The last part draws on the lessons of the earlier parts, making it the most comprehensive. Some lessons are designed to take up a full class period, some are shorter, and some require homework assignments. The teacher will need to determine what is appropriate for his or her class based on allotted time and teaching goals.

c. Primary and Secondary Sources

The historical documents, images, cartoons, and other materials called for in the Classroom Activities are in this section; each piece is designed to be reproduced for the students. In most cases, the teacher will create handouts of these materials; when the sources are used to stimulate class discussions, the teacher can make overheads.

d. Background Material

After the Primary Sources are reference sources, including glossary words, biographies, information on important laws, and descriptions of relevant events. The teacher may wish to make handouts or overheads of this material or write some of the information on the board to help students with unfamiliar vocabulary or concepts.

4. ADDITIONAL RESOURCES

The end of each book highlights three additional ways students can further their research of the general topic. The Integrating National History Day overview presents ideas for student projects and demonstrates how the topics in the book can support them. Next is Using the ABC-CLIO Web Sites for Researching Native American Resistance, a brief description of the ways the ABC-CLIO Web sites can help students narrow their topics, identify relevant sources, and analyze what they find. Finally, there is a section listing additional topic ideas related to the resource book titles that students might be interested in studying.

We hope you find this format user-friendly and that you are able to adapt it easily to fit your students' needs.

Preface

For young adults, it is simply not enough to read texts about vital issues at the heart of American citizenship. Like the generations before them, today's students are going to grapple with these topics in their lifetimes. They need to prepare by turning a critical eye on the histories of uncivil disobedience, Native American resistance, and the environmental movement. Their understanding of the past will help them to make sense of the present and to make informed decisions in the future. Teaching students to examine these issues as they relate to the theme of *The Individual in History* will provide a framework from which to push past the antiquated view of history as mere facts and dates and delve down into historical content to develop perspective and understanding.

Students sometimes learn history quickly and neglect analyses of meaning. The discipline is vast, and the current educational climate emphasizes coverage of content over depth. Class design is often determined by time periods and approached chronologically. Without a guiding framework, however, students are relegated to learning isolated pieces of historical information. A theme redefines how history is learned. Instead of concentrating on an entire century or a broad topic, students are asked to stop and analyze a smaller event, a part of the story, and place it in the context of the whole. Teaching with a theme ensures that students are not overwhelmed by the sheer vastness of the field but are instead invited to look deeply into a manageable portion of it.

The Individual in History provides students with a lens through which they can examine history, an organizational structure that helps them to place information in the correct context and gives them the ability to see connections through time. We invite your students to extend their study of uncivil disobedience, Native American resistance, and the environmental movement by engaging in active research and presentation.

Reconsidering
Resistance

Reconsidering Resistance

AUTHOR

DR. JOHN P. BOWES
Eastern Kentucky University

Native American Resistance uses the examples of two time periods and places—colonial New England and the early 19th-century Ohio Valley—and three individuals—King Philip (the name the English gave to Metacomet), Tecumseh, and Tenskwatawa—to examine how native peoples in North America negotiated their relationship with European colonists and American citizens. The essays, exercises, and documents that follow explore the reasons for, as well as the means and legacies of, Native American resistance to the physical and cultural invasion of their lands and lives. This is a history that has most often been dominated by conflict, and violence has been viewed as the only or final alternative for native peoples. But even as this resource book focuses on two eras of conflict, it asks us to reconsider the notion of resistance and sets forth some basic questions: What led Native Americans to violent resistance and what other options were available and viable?

The first part of *Native American Resistance* centers on colonial New England and the actions of the Wampanoag leader King Philip. This focus serves two purposes. First and most important, it provides insight into the causes of the uprising in 1675 known as King Philip's War. Second, it examines the impact of the first 50 years of English colonization on the native peoples of New England. The second part of this resource book shifts the focus west into the Ohio Valley in the early 1800s. In that place and time, two Shawnee Indian brothers, Tecumseh and Tenskwatawa, inspired and led an Indian confederacy against the growing presence of American citizens and American government in their world. Yet, even as the brothers worked together, their individual beliefs and choices illustrated different ways to deal with American expansion.

Resistance is a much more flexible word than many people give it credit for. The multiple meanings include opposition to somebody or something and the ability to remain unaltered by the invasive and harmful effects of an outside force. This resource book, therefore, presents an opportunity to expand our understanding of not only how and why Native Americans resisted but also what it meant to resist the presence and culture of Europeans and Americans over the course of several centuries.

▲ Native American leader Metacomet, also known as King Philip. King Philip's War, in terms of numbers engaged and casualties sustained, was the single bloodiest Indian war in American history. Though King Philip showed diplomatic finesse by uniting with other tribes, it was a war that he could not win. His defeat presaged the ultimate removal of Native Americans from the New England region. (Library of Congress)

The Reasons for Resistance

Colonial and early American history can be described as a process through which a Native American landscape was transformed into an American nation. During a critical period from the 1600s to the 1800s, European colonists and their descendants redrew the boundaries and

► Powhatan was the principal chief of the so-called Powhatan Confederacy in Virginia during the late 16th and early 17th centuries. (Library of Congress)

redefined everyday life on this continent. The role of native peoples in the creation of the United States is a critical element of that story. And although it may initially appear to be a question with an obvious answer, it helps to ask why native peoples resisted these developments.

The first part of the answer rests in the attitude of European colonists, who often neglected diplomacy in favor of displays of strength. Powhatan, the father of Pocahontas and the Pamunkey Indian leader who faced off against the English at Jamestown, addressed this point in a speech made to John Smith in 1609. "What will it availe you to take that by force you may quickly have by love," he asked, "or to destroy them that provide you food" (Calloway 1994, 38). In light of Powhatan's critique, native resistance may therefore at times be understood as a response to a European approach based on force over friendship.

The manner of colonization also played a significant role in the decision made by native peoples to resist. Most colonists of 17th-century New England and American frontierspeople in the early 19th-century Ohio Valley did not envision a place for Indians in the future of those respective regions. The Wampanoags, Narragansetts, Shawnees, and other Indian peoples were viewed more as obstacles than as neighbors. Those Indians who chose to resist often believed conflict was the only way to counteract such an extreme position.

Finally, we must address the beliefs colonists imposed in their encounters. Europeans determined that the Indians had only two options—to accommodate Western civilization or resist with violence. In short, Indians could abandon their traditional way of life or they could fight to the death. Either way, most Europeans expected Indians to disappear from the landscape. Those Indians who chose resistance decided that possible death was more acceptable than discarding their culture and traditions.

The lives of King Philip, Tecumseh, and Tenskwatawa reflect elements of all of this. By 1675, King Philip and his Wampanoag people lived in a world that had changed dramatically since the *Mayflower* crossed the Atlantic 55 years earlier. Their land base had substantially diminished, and the Puritan leaders of the Massachusetts Bay and Plymouth colonies sought to control the lives of Indians in the region. In the early 19th century, Tecumseh and Tenskwatawa reacted to both the encroachment of American settlers in the Great Lakes region and the negative

▲ A Shawnee mystic and the brother of Tecumseh, Tenskwatawa was the first of two influential Indians to be called the Prophet, appointing himself prophet in 1805. Laulewasika was his given name, but he adopted the name Elkswatawa, and later Tenskwatawa, the Shawnee Prophet. (Hulton Archive/Getty Images)

influences of American culture among their people. None of the three men believed their continued existence should depend on their acceptance of American civilization.

Resistance and Accommodation

Just as important as the reasons for resistance are the ways in which Native American resistance has been discussed over the years. In the narrative of American history, from the colonial period to the present, historians have presented Native Americans and their actions in a simplistic manner. Scholars have reflected the attitudes of the past and have given Native Americans two choices. They could either resist or accommodate. The most glaring evidence of this trend rests in those Native Americans most familiar to Americans today. If asked, most people can recite a list of names that includes Sitting Bull, Geronimo, Crazy Horse, Tecumseh, Pocahontas, and Sacagawea. It is a list that can be divided quite easily between those who chose to fight and those who chose to help the Europeans and Americans they encountered.

Yet rarely, if ever, was the choice so simple, and the lives of those men and women included more than acts of violence or accommodation. Sitting Bull's story does not begin and end with his defeat of George Armstrong Custer at the Battle of the Little Big Horn. Nor can the full experience of Sacagawea be captured in the role she played during Lewis and Clark's western expedition. In short, these respective acts of violent resistance and peaceful accommodation are only moments in time. They do not define the lives of these individuals and they do not reveal the only options available to Sitting Bull and Sacagawea.

The contents of this resource book illustrate a number of ways to discuss the more complicated factors at work in resistance. The records from colonial New England present both long- and short-term causes of King Philip's War and give voice to English and Native American explanations for the uprising. Documents from the early 1800s allow us to hear from Tecumseh, Tenskwatawa, and their native and nonnative opponents. All of these records flesh out events and decisions that defy a simple choice

▲ General Custer, with a few armed soldiers of the 7th Cavalry, surrounded by Native American Lakota Sioux, Crow, Northern, and Cheyenne at the Little Big Horn Battlefield on June 26, 1876, in Little Big Horn River, Montana. (Western History/Genealogy Dept., Denver Public Library.)

between resistance and accommodation. More important, they provide insight into the various definitions of resistance.

The Means of Resistance

Perhaps it is most important to recognize that discussions of Native American resistance cannot be limited in scope to violent encounters alone. As already noted, the very definition of resistance is far more flexible. Over the past 400 years and more, native peoples have opposed the intrusion of Europeans and Americans through violent, legal, and cultural means.

▲ Attack on the Great Swamp Fortress during King Philip's War in 1675. The Great Swamp Fortress was a Narragansett stronghold near present-day South Kingston, Rhode Island, which served as a place of refuge from the expanding pressures of the English colonists until it was burned in 1675. (North Wind Picture Archives)

The violence of both the Pequot War and King Philip's War overshadows the other ways in which the native communities of New England attempted to deal with Puritan colonists in the 1600s. One notable example occurred in 1644, when the Narragansett Indians sent a petition to King Charles I of England. The Narragansett people had witnessed the destruction of the Pequots less than a decade earlier and believed they needed protection. In their petition, they declared themselves to be subjects of the king, a move that would place them under the protection of the king and on equal footing with the Puritans, who were also English subjects. It was a clever attempt to have the king protect them from his other subjects. Although the petition failed, it proved that the Narragansett leaders understood that there was more than one available option to protect their people and their lands.

In a similar fashion, the military confederacy built by Tecumseh tends to marginalize the religious revitalization movement initiated by his brother. Tenskwatawa, the Shawnee Prophet, did not see violent resistance as the only means for resisting American expansion. From his perspective, the strength of the Shawnee Indians rested in returning to their traditional way of life and rejecting the harmful European and American influences. This movement of cultural revitalization is just one example of many from the 1600s to the 1900s, as Native American prophets and leaders sought ways to promote cultural integrity among their people.

The Legacy of Resistance

The three individuals discussed in this resource book represent an interesting array when it comes to legacy and memory. Tecumseh has the greatest name recognition, although New England residents are more likely to know about King Philip. Tenskwatawa is a slightly different story. Residents of the Ohio Valley are most likely to know of the Shawnee Prophet, but few will recognize his actual name.

A number of circumstances explain their different legacies, but perhaps nothing accounts for those differences better than the emphasis on violent resistance in the history of encounters between Europeans and Americans on one side and Native Americans on the other side. Few know more about King Philip than the fact that his English name (King Philip) is attached to a war. Tecumseh is remembered as a valiant figure, a hero who died fighting for the lives of his Shawnee people. Tenskwatawa is remembered more for his military failures than for his religious visions.

▶ A 1645 portrait of a 23-year-old Algonquin man wearing necklace and head ornaments and having facial markings. (Library of Congress)

By learning more about the context of these men's lives, we are able to move beyond those simple legacies. Just as important, we escape the traditional structure of American historical narrative and begin to ask questions about the reasons for, approach to, and consequences of Native resistance.

Sources

Colin G. Calloway, editor, *The World Turned Upside Down: Indian Voices from Early America* (New York: Bedford/St. Martin's, 1994).

R. David Edmunds, *The Shawnee Prophet* (Lincoln: University of Nebraska Press, 1983).

Gregory Evans Dowd, *A Spirited Resistance: The North American Indian Struggle for Unity, 1745–1815* (Baltimore: Johns Hopkins University Press, 1992).

Jill Lepore, *The Name of War: King Philip's War and the Origins of American Identity* (New York: Vintage Books, 1998).

From Colonial America to Today

From Colonial America to Today

AUTHOR

**DR. JOHN
P. BOWES**
*Eastern Kentucky
University*

Native American resistance has taken many forms during the course of U.S. history. Although it is impossible in this resource book to examine all of the encounters from the colonial era to the present, it is worthwhile to discuss the most prominent events and the approaches taken by native peoples. For organizational purposes, this essay is divided into four chronological sections. However, the events discussed within each section also reflect the points presented in the introductory essay. No single strategy was used by Native Americans to resist the invasive forces of Europeans and white Americans. Instead, over the past four centuries and longer, native peoples have developed and tried numerous means to promote and protect their lands, communities, and cultures.

Colonial America

A brief overview of the colonial American period illustrates two important points. First, although the narrative of U.S. history tends to map the origins of the United States as beginning at the Atlantic seaboard and moving west, colonization occurred from multiple directions and in multiple places on the continent. This resource book examines Native American resistance in colonial New England. But it is helpful to view that resistance in comparison to events like the Pueblo Revolt in 1680. A second important point is that the Native American resistance in each region shaped the nature and effectiveness of European colonization.

The official seal of Massachusetts Bay Colony was created in 1629, the same year the colony itself was established. This seal bears the image of a nearly naked native man. He is holding a bow in one hand and an arrow in the other, and he is saying, "Come over and help us." Based on events of the decades that followed, it is nearly impossible to overstate how misguided that message was. The native peoples of New England had not asked for help, and most Puritan colonists did not make an effort to provide it. The thousands of English settlers who arrived in the region beginning in 1629 were more interested in obtaining land.

▲ John Eliot preaches to Native Americans. Eliot, a member of the Massachusetts Bay Colony during the 17th century, was the first missionary to convert the area's native people. (Library of Congress)

This emphasis on land acquisition dominated the relationship between the Puritans and local Native Americans for most of the 1600s. In 1621, the Wampanoag sachem Massasoit signed a peace treaty with William Bradford and the Pilgrims of Plymouth Colony. Fifty-four years later, another Wampanoag sachem named Metacomet, but known to the English as King Philip, led his people in a war against the descendants of those Pilgrims and their neighbors to the north. Between 1621 and 1675, the Puritans had assumed control over the landscape and attempted to assert control over the lives of the Wampanoags, Pequots, and others. King Philip and his people turned to war at a time when they believed the Puritans had gone too far.

▲ View of Taos Pueblo homes in Taos, New Mexico. Taos Pueblo is the only contemporary Native American community that has been designated both a World Heritage Site and a National Historic Landmark. (iStockPhoto.com)

In 1680, only four years after the end of King Philip's War, more than 15,000 Pueblo Indians rose up and forced the Spanish out of New Mexico. The Pueblo Revolt highlighted both short- and long-term frustrations related to the Spanish presence in the region. For 80 years, Spanish Franciscan friars had assaulted all aspects of Pueblo culture, and a revival of traditional religious practices in the 1670s inspired the Pueblos to rid their lands of the Spanish Catholic presence. Their successful revolt was short-lived, however, because the Spanish returned in force in the 1690s. But they returned with a measure of humility. In particular, the Spanish instituted several policies to protect the legal, political, and religious rights of the Pueblos in New Mexico. Native resistance did not eliminate the outside presence, but the Pueblo Revolt altered the substance of Spanish colonization.

In both large and small ways, native peoples resisted the presence of Spanish, English, and French colonists during the 18th century. Even as conflicts between the European powers on the American continent threatened to engulf native communities, resistance continued. The Iroquois, for example, used their geographic position and diplomatic experience to counteract British and French political interests. Skillful diplomacy enabled the Iroquois to maintain a measure of cultural and geographical integrity, but their balancing act also depended on the presence of multiple powers. The American Revolution dramatically altered that landscape.

The 19th Century

Events of the 1800s revealed continuities in both American expansion and Native American resistance. The key difference was that native peoples had to deal with citizens and representatives of the United States. No longer could the Iroquois and others manipulate European colonial desires. Yet the absence of multiple powers did not result in a singular approach to resistance. Even as the passage of time appeared to signal defeat after defeat, the different avenues of Native American resistance demonstrated the strength and will of native peoples to survive the American onslaught.

A pair of conflicts and revitalization movements provide bookends to the 19th century. In the first decade of the 1800s, the Shawnee Prophet rallied Indians of the Great Lakes region to his vision of a world without white influences and white people. Tecumseh used the power of that vision to build a confederacy he hoped would span the eastern half of the continent. Then in the 1880s, from the Great Basin to the Northern Plains, Native American men and women participated in the Ghost Dance. Inspired by the visions of a Paiute Indian named Wovoka, the Ghost Dance promoted an apocalyptic change that would bring back the buffalo and remove Americans from the landscape. This message of hope and cultural revitalization inspired thousands of western Indians who

▲ An Arapaho Ghost Dance, photographed ca. 1900 by famed ethnologist James Mooney, Jr. The Ghost Dance movement spread westward before its defeat in South Dakota at the Wounded Knee Massacre in 1890. (National Archives)

had suffered from the devastating impact of warfare and settler invasion on the Plains.

At both ends of the century, these paired movements failed to halt the influence and invasion of American culture and the American people. But both examples illustrate that Native Americans continued to believe in approaches beyond violence. Some may view the Ghost Dance as the expression of a desperate people who had seen all of their efforts to protect their lands and cultures fail in the face of overwhelming force.

However, we must recognize that the Ghost Dance was also a critical expression of persistence and resistance. Despite the physical and cultural assaults of the 1800s, thousands of American Indians in the West still believed their cultures and worldviews remained the foundation of their survival.

But not all resistance relied on violence or cultural revitalization. Native peoples in the 19th century also fought American expansion and authority through institutional means like the legal system. Two cases reveal both the legitimacy of legal resistance and the harmful consequences of government inaction during this period. In 1832, in *Worcester v. Georgia,* the Cherokee Nation contested Georgia's claims of authority over a sovereign Indian nation. Yet when the U.S. Supreme Court ruled in favor of the Cherokees, President Andrew Jackson and the federal government refused to enforce the decision. In 1866, the U.S. Supreme Court decided that the state government of Kansas did not have the right to impose taxes on the allotted lands of Shawnee Indians. Unfortunately, this ruling in *Charles Bluejacket v. The Commissioners of Johnson County* came too late to save the lands of those who had lost property due to unpaid taxes.

On the one hand, the 1800s encompassed a series of failures. Regardless of the strategies used, it appeared that the native peoples living within the United States could not halt the invasion of their lands and the assault on all aspects of their lives. However, the varied approaches to resistance laid the groundwork for future struggles.

▲ This anonymous political cartoon, titled "Andrew Jackson as Great Father," appeared as a satirical comment shortly after the Indian Removal Act was ratified. (Clements Library, University of Michigan)

The 20th Century

Although the Native American population reached its lowest point at the dawn of the 20th century, native peoples and cultures still existed within the United States. And by the time another 100 years had passed, Native Americans had made an unprecedented recovery. This resurgence illustrates the importance and success of their efforts to resist the ongoing attacks of American government and society on their lands, cultures, and identities.

From 1900 to 2000, resistance seldom led to bloodshed, although the confrontational politics of the American Indian Movement sparked incidents of violence. But episodes like the occupation of Alcatraz in 1969 and Wounded Knee in 1973 were intended to be dramatic and symbolic. Native activists used confrontation as a means to highlight the injustices faced by reservation and urban Indians, and their approach represented a new brand of Native American resistance. It was an opposition developed by native peoples who had a greater familiarity with American society and were intent on having their voices heard.

Land remained the most contested resource. Although the allotment policy begun in 1887 decimated Indian land holdings into the 1920s, native leaders and communities proved resilient. They took advantage of government policies like the Indian Claims Commission and fought to retain and recover a land base that would enable them to maintain their respective communities. Even in victory, however, some tribes refused to compromise their cultural integrity. To this day, members of the Sioux Nation have refused to sign documents that would grant them access to hundreds of millions of dollars. A 1980 Supreme Court ruling awarded that money to pay for the Black Hills and other South Dakota lands taken unjustly in the 19th century. But the Sioux Nation will not take the money and insists that the government return the land.

This stand is a reflection of a larger struggle among native peoples to maintain their identity in the face of an ongoing cultural assault. A similar conflict is evident in the work of Native American intellectuals. The first decades of the 20th century saw the rise to prominence of a group of Native American men and women who had attended government-funded boarding schools and were able to address American society with familiarity. Charles Eastman, a Dakota Sioux Indian who attended Dartmouth College and Boston University, spoke out about the need for Indians to obtain a "white man's" education. Some of his peers disagreed and argued that native peoples needed to resist the lure of American society so as not to abandon their cultures and communities.

▲ Charles Eastman, a Sioux Indian, championed Native American causes from the time of the Wounded Knee Massacre in 1890 until his death in 1939. His writings interpreted Native American ways of life for white Americans during a time of much misunderstanding, and his work served the cause of his people in many ways. (Library of Congress)

▲ A tipi is erected on Alcatraz to symbolize the claim to native lands during the Native American occupation of the island in November, 1969. A group called the Indians of All Tribes occupied the island until 1971, residing in abandoned buildings and living off food ferried over from mainland San Francisco. The protest was one of the more dramatic events of the ongoing Native American rights movement. (Bettmann/ Corbis)

By the late 1900s, Native American intellectuals like Vine Deloria, Jr., had taken a stronger stance in defense of native cultures. In books like *Custer Died for Your Sins,* Deloria aggressively promoted native identities and attacked the damaging legacy of federal policies and American attitudes. Deloria, and other prominent Native American activists and intellectuals, found it necessary to declare even the most fundamental concept—that Native Americans continued to exist within the United States. In a country where images of Indians served as caricatures and mascots for sports teams, these Native American men and women recognized that they had to fight battles on numerous fronts to look out for the interests of their people and their communities.

The 21st Century

Because the 21st century is less than a decade old, any new approaches to resistance are still developing. However, the battlegrounds are clear, primarily because the same issues remain at the center of U.S.–Indian relations. Most important is the principle of sovereignty. In the legal system, political negotiations, and daily life, native nations have to defend and promote their sovereign relationship with the U.S. government. But they do so from a position that grows more powerful every day. Native activists and leaders have helped create national legislation to repatriate Native American remains and material goods to their respective communities. Among some native nations, the revenue from gaming has funded projects to build homes, start businesses, and preserve languages.

Over more than four centuries, native peoples have resisted attempts to remove them and their cultures from the landscape of this continent. And though episodes like King Philip's War and Tecumseh and Tenskwatawa's pan-Indian movement appear to demonstrate failed attempts of the past, they clearly reveal more than defeat. Since the arrival of Europeans, both the failures and successes of Native American resistance laid the foundation for the continued presence and strength of native nations in the present.

Sources

John P. Bowes, *Exiles and Pioneers: Eastern Indians in the Trans-Mississippi West* (New York: Cambridge University Press, 2007).

Colin G. Calloway, *First Peoples: A Documentary Survey of American Indian History,* 3rd edition (New York: Bedford/St. Martins, 2007).

Vine Deloria, Jr., *Custer Died for Your Sins: An Indian Manifesto* (Norman: University of Oklahoma, 1988).

R. David Edmunds, *Tecumseh and the Quest for Indian Leadership* (New York: Pearson Longman, 2006).

Frederick E. Hoxie, *Talking Back to Civilization: Indian Voices from the Progressive Era* (New York: Bedford/St. Martins, 2001).

Peter Iverson, *"We Are Still Here": American Indians in the Twentieth Century* (Wheeling, IL: Harlan Davidson, 1998).

Jill Norgren, *The Cherokee Cases: Two Landmark Federal Decisions in the Fight for Sovereignty* (Norman: University of Oklahoma Press, 2004).

Jeffrey Ostler, *The Plains Sioux and U.S. Colonialism from Lewis and Clark to Wounded Knee* (New York: Cambridge University Press, 2004).

King Philip and New England Colonial Expansion in the 1670s

King Philip and New England Colonial Expansion in the 1670s

▲ Powhatan was the principal chief of the so-called Powhatan Confederacy in Virginia during the late 16th and early 17th centuries. (Library of Congress)

The arrival of European settlers in the New World was the impetus for numerous conflicts in North America during early colonial times. A prime example was the Anglo-Powhatan Wars in Virginia, which began in 1609 after the founding of Jamestown and continued for decades. Farther north in New England, the English settlers who established Plymouth (1620) and Boston (1630) also found themselves involved in hostilities with Native American tribes. Additional settlements were established by English colonists throughout the region, much to the alarm of the various eastern Algonquian Indian tribes in New England. A series of incidents during the 1630s culminated in the first significant conflict between the two sides—the Pequot War (1636–1638), which resulted in the destruction of the Pequots by the English settlers.

The relationship between English colonists and American Indians in New England continued to deteriorate after the Pequot War. By the mid-17th century, many of the colonial leaders who had forged a working relationship with the eastern Algonquian tribes in the region had died, and a new generation of leaders proved to be less inclined to accommodate their Native American neighbors. Likewise, some key Indian elders who had negotiated with the early New England colonists had also passed away, most notably the Wampanoag chief Massasoit, who had signed the Massasoit Peace Treaty with the Plymouth settlers in 1621. Both sides worked hard to maintain peace throughout Massasoit's life, despite bitter conflicts between Indians and colonists in other parts of New England. After Massasoit died in 1662, his eldest son, Wamsutta, struggled to keep the peace. Later that year, Wamsutta died on his way home after being interrogated by colonial authorities from Plymouth, and his brother Metacomet (known as King Philip), took over as sachem. King Philip, who believed Wamsutta was poisoned by the English, took a much harder line against settlers moving into the region.

◀ Native American leader Meta-comet, also known as King Philip. King Philip's War, in terms of numbers engaged and casualties sustained, was the single bloodiest Indian war of American history. Though King Philip showed diplomatic finesse by uniting with other tribes, it was a war that he could not win. His defeat presaged the ultimate removal of Native Americans from the New England region. (Library of Congress)

For the next decade, King Philip maneuvered to maintain his power and ensure his people's welfare as the English population, and power, expanded. Wampanoag holdings formed the borders of Plymouth colony, Rhode Island, and the Massachusetts Bay settlement, and each wanted the area. King Philip sold tracts of land to various colonists in an attempt to maintain his influence in the region. Subsequent conflicts over colonial borders were rarely settled to King Philip's satisfaction—colonial courts seemed biased and unwilling to rule in the Indians' favor. The Wampanoags were also angered by colonial efforts to shape native politics, and additional tensions arose as English livestock wandered into Indian fields, destroying crops.

▲ In one of the largest battles of King Philip's War, General Geoff leads the colonists to defeat a Pequot attack at Hadley Mountain. (Library of Congress)

King Philip began using money from the sale of land to stock up on firearms. John Sassamon, a Christian Indian and former aide to King Philip who was acting as an ambassador for the English, informed the colonial authorities in Plymouth that King Philip was gearing up for war. Sassamon was soon found murdered, and the English colonists executed three Wampanoags for the crime in June 1675, igniting King Philip's War.

The conflict began in July 1675, when angry groups of Wampanoags carried out raids against English settlements in the area, leading to a full-scale uprising. The English colonists opted for a defensive strategy, although such individuals as Benjamin Church advocated for a more aggressive policy. Church was eventually allowed to adopt Indian tactics and achieved notable success with that strategy. After failing to defeat King Philip, the United Colonies, led by Plymouth governor Josiah Winslow, chose to attack the formidable Narragansetts during the winter of 1675–1676. The colonists crushed the Narragansett tribe during the Great Swamp Fight on December 19, 1675, and the remaining Narragansetts formed an alliance with the Wampanoags. King Philip continued his raids in early 1676, including an attack on Lancaster, Massachusetts, during which his forces captured Mary Rowlandson. Rowlandson's captivity narrative about her experience became a frontier classic when it was published in 1682.

By the spring of 1676, King Philip's situation had deteriorated, as attacks on his army by Mohawks allied with colonial New York and disease and hunger took their toll on his men. Around that same time, the Native American alliances he forged fell apart as many Indians moved north and west to escape the fighting or made peace with the colonies. In August 1676, King Philip and his dwindling forces were surrounded in the Assowamset Swamp in Rhode Island, and he was shot and killed by an Indian serving with colonial forces. King Philip's War decimated the American Indian population of southern New England, and King Philip's death marked the end of Native American independence in the region.

King Philip and New England Colonial Expansion in the 1670s

AUTHOR

CHRIS MULLIN
Santa Ynez Valley
Union High School

AUTHOR

BRETT PIERSMA
Santa Ynez Valley
Union High School

This section of the resource book will focus primarily on the 17th century in New England and will take place in four stages. The primary focus will be on political and military conflicts between King Philip (Metacomet) and the English colonists in the region. The unit will also trace the experiences of Englishwoman Mary Rowlandson as revealed through her captivity narrative.

Lesson 1 In this lesson, students will recreate a military event in writing by deciphering a primary source sketch of the battle. They will then compare their conjecture to a historian's description of the battle.

Lesson 2 Next, students will uncover the real causes for King Philip's War by evaluating statements made both by King Philip and an official English investigator. Students will pinpoint their findings by comparing both parties' viewpoints in a Venn diagram.

Lesson 3 In this lesson, students will discover the cultural traits of King Philip's Indian kinspeople as seen through the eyes of Mary Rowlandson, who was their captive. The class will treat Rowlandson's diary entries as a source for anthropological study.

Lesson 4 To conclude, students will participate in a strategic board game that mimics the regions and movement of Indian and English soldiers in King Philip's War. Students will gain insight into the difficulties of scoring an easy victory.

LESSON 1
Anatomy of a Battlefield

MATERIALS NEEDED

HANDOUTS

- Instructions for Analyzing Scenes from the Pequot War, p. 32
- Mystic Fort Fight Overview and Guide Questions, pp. 33–34

ILLUSTRATION

- Scenes from the Pequot War, p. 60

In this opening activity, students will work in pairs to decipher historical evidence and recreate events from 17th-century colonial America. First, the teacher should distribute the illustration, Scenes from the Pequot War. The teacher should explain to students that their task is to play the role of a historical detective who has stumbled on centuries-old evidence. Students should break into pairs and study the primary source, using the Instructions for Analyzing Image of Scenes from the Pequot War handout, to try to assemble a sense of what happened.

Once their curiosity is piqued, the teacher should distribute the Mystic Fort Fight Overview and Guide Questions handout to each pair. This handout provides students with a textual overview of the event, along with a series of questions to guide their work.

Lesson 1, Handout

Instructions for Analyzing Scenes from the Pequot War

Instructions: Look closely at this battle drawing. It is a primary source illustration that appeared in *Newes from America* published by John Underhill in London in 1638. English readers were fascinated by the events, especially the military events, taking place in the colonies.

Working in pairs, take on the role of a historical investigator. Using only the images and words in the picture, see if you can recreate a plausible scenario for this event.

Guide questions:

- Who are the main participants?

- What kind of event is taking place?

- What are the main features of the battlefield? Structures? Topography? Other elements?

- Who is leading the attack?

- What do you think is the outcome of the battle?

- What kind of weapons and clothing were used?

- Why are Native Americans inside and outside the attack area?

- Write a single paragraph that describes your view of what happened here.

Lesson 1, Handout
Mystic Fort Fight Overview and Guide Questions

Instructions: Now that you have completed an initial deciphering of the illustration, read the following description to find out what really happened in this depicted event.

This illustration depicts the assault on a Pequot community near the Mystic River in Connecticut on May 26, 1637. The attack was carried out by a force of English settlers and Native American allies consisting of the Narragansetts and Mohegans against Pequot Indians. Pequot warriors had raided Wethersfield, an English settlement, killing six men, three women, and much livestock, and capturing two girls. The General Court of the Connecticut colony responded by declaring an "offensive war" on the Pequots. It sent 90 men under Captain John Mason on a retaliatory mission. Mason's force arrived at Fort Saybrook accompanied by a number of Mohegan warriors, and there Mason met another smaller group of 20 men under Captain John Underhill from the Massachusetts colony. Mason decided to move his force to Narragansett Bay from where he planned to attack a large fortified Pequot settlement on the Mystic River. On the evening of May 23, 1637, Mason landed with about 70 men from Connecticut, 19 from Massachusetts, and some 70 Mohegan warriors. He negotiated with Narragansett leaders to pass through their lands, and he marched his forces westward the following day. On the morning of May 25, several hundred Narragansett warriors joined Mason's expedition. The men rested during the night and then began their attack around daybreak. The attackers first surrounded the village and fired a musket volley, surprising the sleeping Pequots inside. Then, divided into two forces—one each under Mason and Underhill—the men simultaneously assaulted the two entrances in the palisade. The Pequots defended themselves with bows and arrows and in hand-to-hand combat. Although the original English intention was to kill the inhabitants, the attackers found the struggle difficult in the tight quarters among the Pequot wigwams, leading their commanders to decide to set fire to the village. The large fire soon engulfed the settlement; numerous Pequots died in the blaze and many warriors fought to the last. Other Pequots fled the village, but almost all those attempting to escape were slain by the English or their Native American allies. English casualities for the campaign amounted to 2 killed and 20 hurt. Estimates of Pequots slain at Mystic range from 400 to 700 people. Mason claimed that only seven were taken captive and seven escaped.

Continues on next page

Lesson 1, Handout

Mystic Fort Fight Overview and Guide Questions, Continued

Instructions: Working with your same partner, answer the following questions:

- What tribes fought alongside the English against the Pequots?

- What colonies were working together to wage war on the Pequots?

- What started the war?

- In what colony was the battle?

- How did each side do in the battle?

- Was your paragraph in step 1 accurate about any of the events? Which ones?

- Are you surprised that Indians fought alongside the English against other Indians?

- What are the limitations to working with an image like this to interpret history?

- Do you think this picture shows "bias" or the unfair treatment of one of groups by the artist? Why? Why not?

LESSON 2
The Causes of King Philip's War

MATERIALS NEEDED

EXCERPTS FOR INDIVIDUAL STUDENT WORK

- *King Philip's War,* Report by Edward Randolph, pp. 61–64

EXCERPTS FOR SMALL GROUP WORK

- Excerpt 1, *King Philip's War,* Report by Edward Randolph, p. 65
- Excerpt 2, *King Philip's War,* Report by Edward Randolph, p. 65
- Excerpt 3, *King Philip's War,* Report by Edward Randolph, p. 66
- Excerpt 4, *King Philip's War,* Report by Edward Randolph, p. 66
- Excerpt 5, *King Philip's War,* Report by Edward Randolph, p. 67
- Excerpt 6, *King Philip's War,* Report by Edward Randolph, p. 67

EXCERPT FOR WHOLE CLASS ACTIVITY

- *A Relation of the Indian War,* by John Easton, p. 68

This lesson takes place in two parts, looking at the causes of King Philip's War in Massachusetts in 1685 from two different perspectives. Students will uncover the real causes of the war, first by evaluating statements made by an official English investigator who was dispatched by the London government to report on the events in the colonies, then by examining King Philip's perspective.

The teacher should photocopy the excerpts for individual student work, *King Philip's War,* Report by Edward Randolph, which includes 27 short excerpts taken from Edward Randolph's original report on the causes of the war. Each student in the class should receive one quote (if there are more than 27 students in the class, 2 students may receive the same quote; if there are fewer, students can receive more than one). The teacher should tell the students that they are going to be studying an episode in American history and that they will be using primary sources to discover what happened.

The students should be instructed to mingle around the room taking turns reading their quotes to each other. They should move quickly so that they can hear as many quotes as possible. After an appropriate amount of time, the teacher should ask students to return to their seats, then guide them in brainstorming what they think is happening.

Some possible guide questions include the following:

- What kind of event is the document describing?
- When do you think this event took place?
- Where do you think the event happened?
- What interesting phrases or words got your attention?

When the discussion is finished, the teacher should instruct students to reread their excerpts as a class, in order according to the number of each quote. The teacher should ask the class if the document makes more sense now that the sentences are read in order. Students should be invited to share anything new they learned after reading the excerpts in order.

Continues on next page

Lesson 2

The Causes of King Philip's War, Continued

To continue the analysis of Edward Randolph's report, the teacher should write the following three columns on the board, and work with the class to fill in the columns as completely as possible:

- **What I know**
- **What I want/need to know**
- **Hard vocabulary**

Next, students will meet in small groups to discuss longer excerpts of the report and "translate" it into understandable English. The teacher should divide the students into six small groups and distribute one of the Excerpts for Small Group Work to each group. The students' task is to review their excerpt, rewrite it in easy-to-understand language, and then explain its meaning to the class. The teacher can provide dictionaries for difficult words. The groups should present their excerpts in numbered order (1, 2, 3, 4, 5, 6).

To conclude the dissection and analysis of this document, the teacher should create a final chart on the board that lists the various causes of the war, as perceived by Edward Randolph. And before moving on to King Philip's perspective on the causes, the teacher should ask students the following questions:

- Do you think this source is reliable? Why? Why not?
- Does the author seem to take the side of the Indians or the English colonists in Massachusetts? Explain.

Once students have a thorough understanding of Randolph's explanation for the causes of King Philip's War, they will review the causes from King Philip's point of view and compare the two perspectives. The teacher should distribute the excerpt for the whole group discussion, *A Relation of the Indian War* by John Easton. The teacher should point out that in this instance, the views of King Philip are being retold by an Englishman and state to the class:

In the following excerpt, John Easton, attorney general of Rhode Island, describes in his own words the complaints that King Philip (Metacomet) had made against the English colonists. Read this excerpt, which describes King Philip's view of the wrongs that led to the military crisis of 1675–1676. Are King Philip's views (according to John Easton) consistent with those described in the Edward Randolph source? Together, we will read the excerpt aloud (using jump-in or popcorn reading) and will stop periodically to make a list of any complaints King Philip made.

When the class has completed the reading, the teacher should create a large Venn diagram on the board. In the first circle, students should brainstorm all the causes of the war that are unique to the Randolph source, and in the second circle, students should place all the causes unique to the Easton/King Philip document The middle of the diagram should include all the causes both sides agree on.

LESSON 3
Mary Rowlandson's Captivity Narrative

MATERIALS NEEDED

EXCERPTS FROM
MARY ROWLANDSON'S
JOURNAL

- Excerpt 1, p. 69
- Excerpt 2, p. 69
- Excerpt 3, p. 70
- Excerpt 4, p. 70
- Excerpt 5, p. 71
- Excerpt 6, p. 71
- Excerpt 7, p. 72
- Excerpt 8, p. 72
- Excerpt 9, p. 73
- Excerpt 10, p. 74
- Excerpt 11, p. 75
- Excerpt 12, p. 76
- Excerpt 13, p. 77
- Excerpt 14, p. 78
- Excerpt 15, p. 79
- Excerpt 16, p. 80
- Excerpt 17, p. 80

At one point in King Philip's War, Mary Rowlandson was captured during an attack on her town and transported by her Indian captors for some weeks around the New England countryside. Rowlandson wrote a detailed account of her daily life in captivity, and it was a very popular book in its day.

In this activity, students will learn about Native American culture through 17 short selections from Rowlandson's publication. Each student will travel around the classroom and read and take notes on four or five excerpts from her journal.

Before the activity begins, the teacher should place the 17 excerpts in a complete circle around the room. The excerpts should be visible and numbered but do not need to be put in any kind of chronological order. The teacher should divide the students into groups of one or two, so that there is at least one student at each journal entry.

Students should be instructed to read the short entry in front of them and to make a list of all cultural or social insights they glean from the readings. Students should continue, moving to the journal entry to their right a few times, until they have reviewed four to five entries. They should then return to their seats.

To wrap up the lesson, students should share all the interesting cultural facts they discovered on their "travels."

LESSON 4
Simulation of King Philip's War

MATERIALS NEEDED

GAME PIECES

- Game Board, pp. 44–45
- Indian Region Markers, p. 46
- English Region Markers, p. 47
- Indian Troop Markers, p. 48
- English Troop Markers, p. 49

TEACHER'S GUIDES FOR BONUS BATTLES

- Ashguodash Region: Battle of Springfield, p. 50
- Southern Worcester Region: Battle of Brookfield, pp. 51–52
- Marlborough Region: Battle of Lancaster, pp. 53–54
- Great Swamp Region: The Great Swamp Battle, pp. 55–56
- Deerfield Region: Bloody Brook Massacre, pp. 57–58

In this simulation, students will gain insight into the challenges both the English and the Native Americans faced in achieving victory in King Philip's War. Students will play a board game that mimics the regions and movements of Indian and English soldiers during the war. Although this game represents the real historical event, it is also a game of strategy that provides an equal opportunity for either side to win.

Overview

The game board has been divided into 22 different regions, including the colonies of Massachusetts, Rhode Island, and Connecticut. The regions are divided equally between the Indians under King Philip and the English colonial soldiers. The class is divided into two groups: Native Americans and English soldiers. The object of the game is to capture regions from the opponent until one side controls all 22 regions.

During the game each team will use two types of markers, Region Markers and Troop Markers. Region Markers identify which team (Indian or English) occupies a specific region. Each team starts by controlling half (11) of the regions. As regions are won or lost throughout the game, the number of pieces each team holds will change.

The Region Markers represent the resources available to a team, and therefore the number of soldiers it can place in the field. At the start of the simulation, each team will receive one Troop Marker for every two Region Markers it possesses (rounding down, this means that each team will receive five Troop Markers). The game takes place in five stages (five seasons) from one winter to the following winter. Troop Markers are reassigned each winter based on the new number of regions possessed by a team at that time.

The teacher should photocopy the game board and enlarge it if possible. Each team should receive the appropriate 11 Region Markers and five Troop Markers. (The teacher should also make a few additional photocopies of Troop Markers, for use in an optional game activity described after the game instructions.)

Lesson 4

Simulation of King Philip's War, Continued

At the start of the game it is winter, and the English and the Indian teams each control 11 regions. Players should place their region markers in each of the designated regions found on the game board according to the following list.

Indian Regions	**English Regions**
1. Northern Berkshire	1. Essex
2. Southern Berkshire	2. Middlesex
3. Deerfield	3. Lancaster
4. Western Connecticut	4. Marlborough
5. Squakeag	5. Southern Worcester
6. Hopeweir Swamp	6. Providence
7. Ashguodash	7. Coastal Connecticut
8. Wabaquosset	8. Bristol
9. Northern Connecticut	9. Plymouth
10. Nipsachuck	10. Boston
11. Great Swamp	11. Norfolk

The Simulation

Round 1: Winter Deployment

To begin, each team secretly decides on which of its 11 regions it will place its five Troop Markers, and then it designates those positions in writing.

- No team may place more than one Troop Marker in any region space.

- No team may place a Troop Marker in the region of another team.

- Teams must place *all* of their Troop Markers into regions.

Once each team has secretly designated its intended Troop Marker positions in writing, the team members provide the written list to the teacher, "game moderator." The game moderator announces the locations of the Troop Markers and puts them in place on the game board.

Continues on next page

Lesson 4

Simulation of King Philip's War, Continued

Round 2: Spring Campaign

Each team views the locations of all Troop Markers on the game board and makes secret plans to attack various regions occupied by the opposing team. This is an opportunity for the teams to devise a strategy that makes best use of their forces and geographic positions.

Each team makes a list describing which troops will attack which region. For example, the English team might write "Southern Worcester attacks Hopeweir Swamp," and the Indian team might write "Nipsachuck and Great Swamp attack Providence."

As soon as each team has committed to writing its intended attack plan, the team must pass it to the moderator who reveals all battle plans to the class.

Round 3: Summer Campaign

To begin, each team views the new Troop Marker and Region Marker positions based on the spring campaigns. As in Round 2, each team secretly designs new attacks and hands them over to the moderator.

Attack plans, troop movements, and region occupations proceed along the same guidelines as in Round 2. As in Round 2, both teams finish by shifting remaining troops as desired.

Lesson 4

Simulation of King Philip's War, Continued

Round 4: Fall Campaign

This round replicates Rounds 2 and 3. Each team views the new Troop Marker and Region Marker positions based on the summer campaigns. As in Rounds 2 and 3, each team secretly designs new attacks and hands them over to the moderator. Attack plans, troop movements, and region occupations proceed along the same guidelines as in Rounds 2 and 3. As in Rounds 2 and 3, both teams finish by shifting remaining troops as desired.

Round 5: Winter Deployment

This round is very similar to Round 1. Each team begins by removing *all* Troop Markers from the game board.

As before, each team counts the number of Region Markers it now possesses and divides by two to see how many total Troop Markers it may receive this round. As before, students secretly write down the regions into which they will place their Troop Markers, and the moderator announces their positions only when both sides have completed and turned in their lists. These will serve as the beginning troop positions for the new spring campaigns.

DEFINING MOMENT I

Lesson 4

Simulation of King Philip's War, Continued

Guidelines for Battle

Teams may commit *any* number of their five Troop Markers to battle. Attacks must be designed and carried out along the following guidelines:

- Troop Markers may only attack directly adjacent regions, and they cannot attack on a diagonal. (For example, Western Connecticut cannot attack Ashguodash nor can troop reinforcements move that way either.)

- Whichever team has more troop markers attacking a specific region wins the contest and thus control of the region.

- When a team's Troop Marker loses in a battle, it may retreat into one of its own adjacent regions provided there is no Troop Marker already present. If there is no adjacent space to retreat, that Troop Marker is removed from play.

- If any attacking Troop Marker is simultaneously attacked by another region, that Troop Marker *must* stay and defend itself. It can no longer be counted as part of the team's attack plan on another region.

- At the end of the round, the winning team must place a Troop Marker in the newly conquered territory. The marker chosen must be one of those that attacked the region.

- In the case of a tie, control of the region remains unchanged. All Troop Markers remain where they started.

Post-battle Guidelines

Once all battles have been concluded, each team may choose, it if wishes, to shift any or all of its Troop Markers according to the following guidelines:

1. Each team may move any number of its remaining Troop Markers one adjacent space (no diagonal movement.)
2. The space into which the Troop Marker is moved must contain no other Troop Markers.
3. The space into which the Troop Marker is moved must be controlled by the team entering the space.

The spring campaigns are now over and teams must prepare for summer campaigns.

Lesson 4

Simulation of King Philip's War, Continued

Winning the Game

The game continues until one team loses all of its regions. The students will repeat Rounds 1 though 4 with three seasons of campaigns and one season of regrouping and redeployment.

Optional Game Activity

For five of the regions there is a battle description that describes a real event that took place there during the war. The first time an attack is made on that region the teacher should read a short primary or secondary source description of the real battle. Each team should be encouraged to listen carefully to the reading as there will be a quick competition for one bonus Troop Marker. When the reading is completed, the teacher can verbally quiz the two teams in turn using the associated guide questions or designing his or her own questions. The team that answers the most number of questions correctly will receive one bonus Troop Marker to be used for that battle only. Once the battle is over, the temporary bonus Troop Marker is removed from the board. The regions are:

1. Ashguodash Region
2. Southern Worcester Region
3. Marlborough Region
4. Great Swamp Region
5. Deerfield Region

The teacher should refer to the Teacher's Guides for Bonus Battles to conduct this optional part of the game. Each includes a battle description, quiz questions, and answers.

DEFINING MOMENT I

Lesson 4, Game Pieces
Game Board

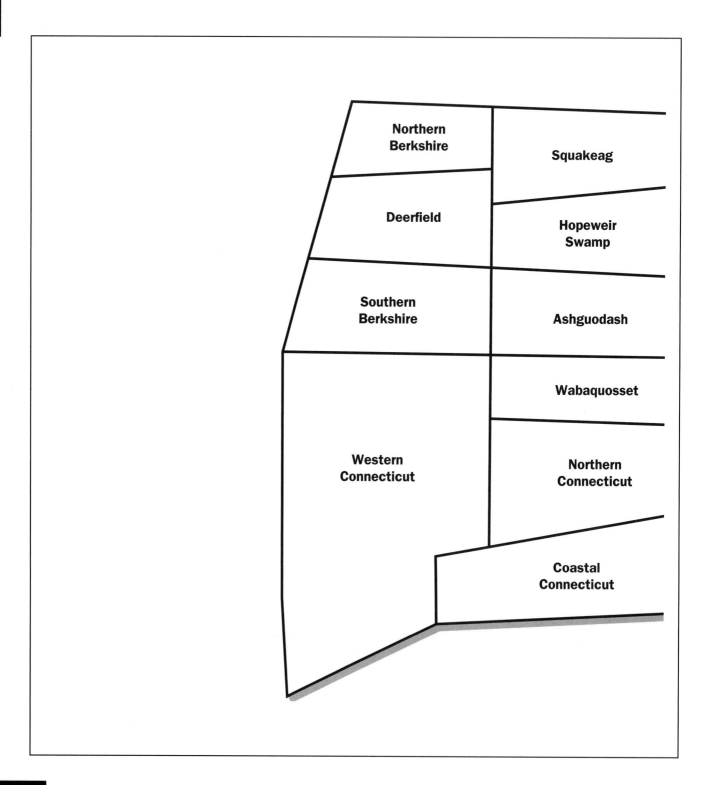

Lesson 4, Game Pieces

Game Board, Continued

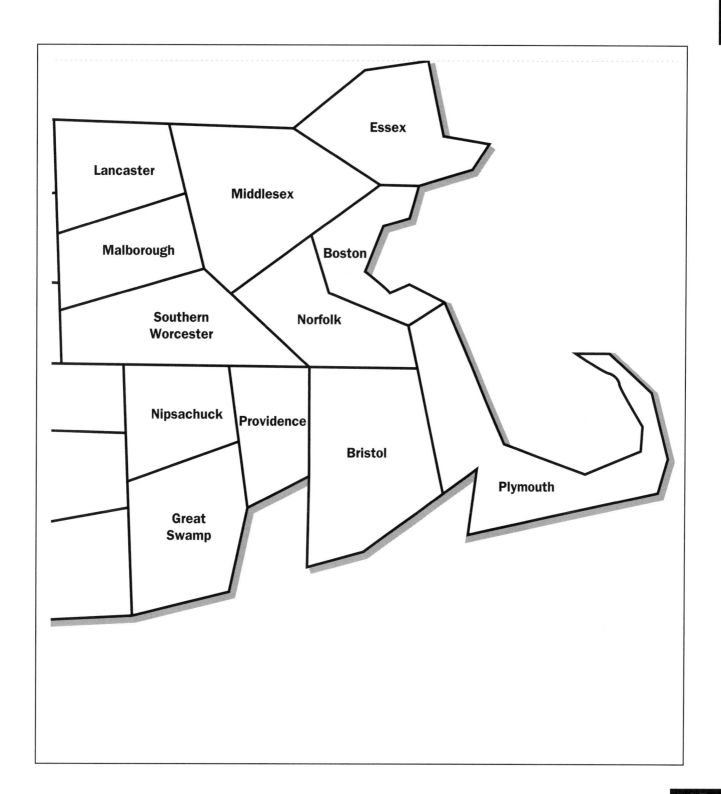

Lesson 4, Game Pieces
Indian Region Markers

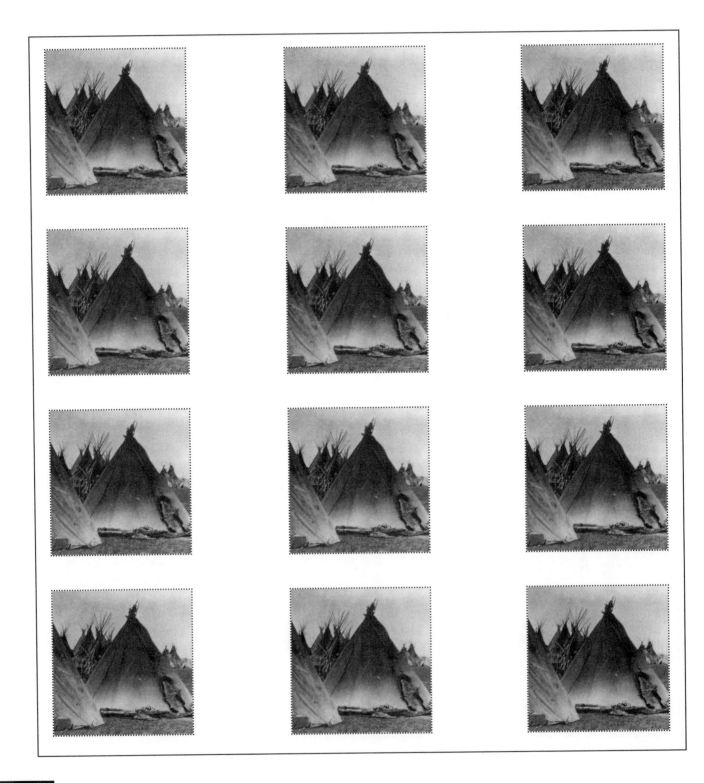

Lesson 4, Game Pieces
English Region Markers

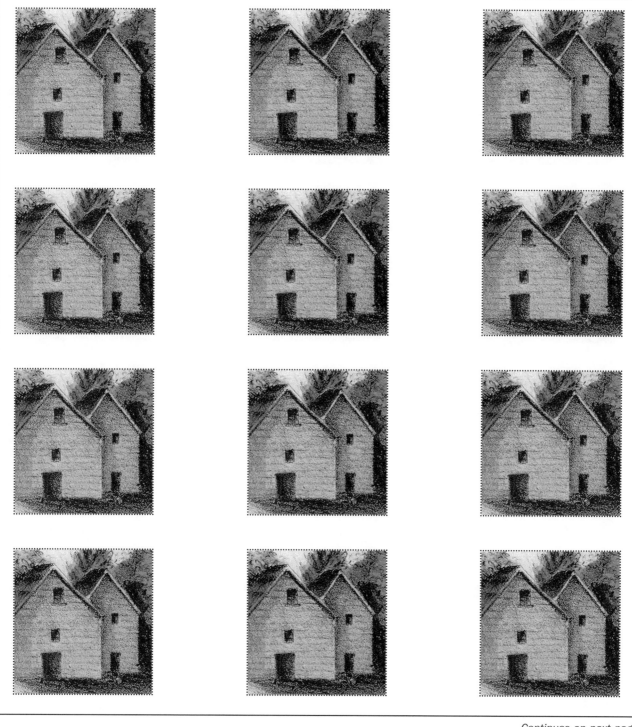

Continues on next page

Lesson 4, Game Pieces
Indian Troop Markers

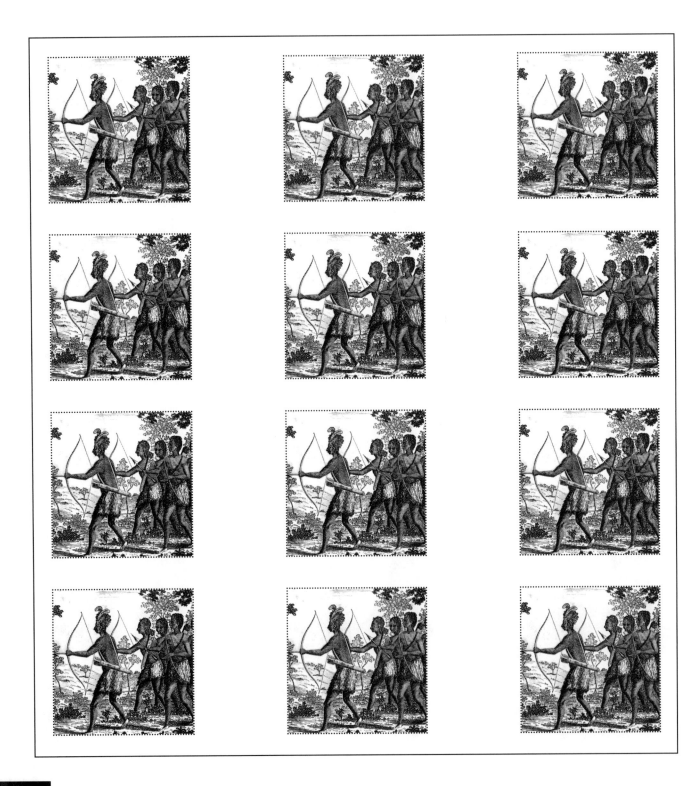

Lesson 4, Game Pieces
English Troop Markers

Lesson 4, Teacher's Guides for Bonus Battle
Ashguodash Region: Battle of Springfield

A Letter to Governor John Leverett from Major John Pynchon

I desire to give you an account of the sore stroke upon poor distressed Springfield, which I hope will excuse my late doing of it. On the 4th of October our soldiers which were at Springfield I had called off, leaving none to secure the town because the Commissioners order was so strict. That night a post was sent to us that 500 Indians were about Springfield intending to destroy it on the 5th of October. With about 200 of our soldiers I marched down to Springfield where we found all in flames, about 30 dwelling houses burnt down and 24 or 25 barns, my corn mill, saw mill, and other buildings. Generally men's hay and corn are burnt, and many men whose houses stand had their goods burnt in other houses which they had carried them to. Lt. Cooper and two more slain and 4 persons wounded. That the town did not utterly perish is cause of great thankfulness. As soon as said forces appeared the Indians drew off, so that we saw none. Our endeavors here are to secure the houses and corn that are left. Our people are under great discouragement and talk of leaving the place. We need your orders and direction about it. How to have provisions, I mean bread, for want of a mill is difficult. The soldiers here already complain on that account, although we have flesh enough. Many of the inhabitants have no houses,which fills and throngs every room of those that have, together with the soldiers; indeed it is very uncomfortable living here. But I resolve to attend what God calls me to and to stick to it as long as I can. I hope God will make up in himself what is wanting in the creature, to me, and to us all.

To speak my thoughts—all these towns ought to be garrisoned, as I have formerly hinted. To go out after the Indians in the swamps and thickets is to hazard all our men, unless we know where they keep, which is altogether unknown to us.

Possible Team Questions

- Q: What town was under attack in this report? A: Springfield

- Q: How many Indians did the English think were present? A: 500

- Q: What caused the Indians to retreat from the town? A: The arrival of English troops

- Q: What kind of property did the author lose? A: His corn mill and his saw mill

- Q: What were the people of the town talking about doing? A: Abandoning the town

- Q: What is the author's fear if the town is abandoned? A: The loss of towns above it as well

- Q: What will be needed to hold the town? A: Many soldiers

Source: Burning of Springfield by the Indians.

Lesson 4, Teacher's Guides for Bonus Battle

Southern Worcester Region: Battle of Brookfield

Captain Thomas Wheeler's Account

The next day being August 3rd, they continued shooting and shouting, and proceeding in their former wickedness, blaspheming the name of the Lord, and reproaching us, his afflicted servants, scoffing at our prayers as they were sending in their shot upon all quarters of the house and many of them went to the town's meeting house . . . who mocked saying, come and pray, and sing psalms, and in contempt made an hideous noise somewhat resembling singing. But we, to our power did endeavor our defense, sending our shot amongst them, the Lord giving us courage to resist them, and preserving us from destruction they sought to bring upon us. . . .They also used several stratagems to fire us, namely, by wild fire in cotton and linen rags with brimstone in them, which rags they tyed to the piles of their arrows, sharp for the purpose, and shot them to the roof of our house, after they had set them on fire, which would have much endangered the burning thereof, had we not used means of cutting holes through the roof, and otherwise, to beat the said arrows down, and God being pleased to prosper our endeavors therin. They carried more combustible matter, as flax and hay, to the sides of the house, and set it on fire, and then flocked apace towards the door of the house, either to prevent our going forth to quench the fire, as we had done before, or to kill our men in their attempt to go forth, or else to break into the house by the door; whereupon we were forced to break down the wall of the house against the fire to put it out. They also shot a ball of wild fire into the garret of the house, which fell amongst a great heap of flax or tow therin, which one of our soldiers, through God's good Providence espyed, and having water ready presently quenched it; and so we were preserved by the keeper of Israel, both our bodies from their shot, which they sent thick against us, and the house from being consumed to ashes, although we were but weak to defend ourselves, we being not above twenty and six men with those of that small town, who were able for any service, and our enemies, as I judged them about . . . three hundred . . . On Wednesday, August the 4th, the Indians fortified themselves at the meeting house, and the barn, belonging to our house, which they fortified both at the great doors, and at both ends, with posts, rails, boards, and hay, to save themselves from our shot. They also devised other stratagems, to fire our house, on the night following, namely, they took a cart, and filled it with flax, hay and candle-wood and other combustible matter, and set up planks, fastened to the cart, to save themselves from the danger of our shot . . . and they loaded the front or fore-end thereof with matter fit for firing, as hay, and flax, and chips, &c. Two of these instruments they prepared, that they might convey fire to the house, with the more safety to themselves, they standing at such a distance from our shot, whilst they wheeled them to the house: . . . But the Lord who is a present help in times of trouble, and is pleased to make his people's extremity his opportunity, did graciously prevent them on effecting what they hoped they should have done by the aforesaid devices, partly by sending a shower of rain in season, whereby the matter prepared being wet would not so easily take fire as it otherwise would have done, and partly by aid coming to our help.

Continues on next page

Lesson 4, Teacher's Guides for Bonus Battle

Southern Worcester Region: Battle of Brookfield, Continued

Possible Team Questions

- Q: What town was under attack in this report? A: Brookfield

- Q: How many Indians did the English think were present? A: 300

- Q: What was the main tactical weapon the Indians were using? A: Fire

- Q: What did the Indians design to bring fire into the fort? A: A wheeled cart

- Q: What stopped the fire from increasing? A: A rainstorm

- Q: Whom does the author thank for saving the town from fire? A: The Lord/God

- Q: How did the English put out a fire besides using water? A: They collapsed a wall on it.

Source: History of the Wheeler Family in America, 1914.

Lesson 4, Teacher's Guides for Bonus Battle
Marlborough Region: Battle of Lancaster

Mary Rowlandson's Account

On the tenth of February 1675, came the Indians with great numbers upon Lancaster: their first coming was about sunrising; hearing the noise of some guns, we looked out; several houses were burning, and the smoke ascending to heaven. There were five persons taken in one house; the father, and the mother and a sucking child, they knocked on the head; the other two they took and carried away alive. There were two others, who being out of their garrison upon some occasion were set upon; one was knocked on the head, the other escaped; another there was who running along was shot and wounded, and fell down; he begged of them his life, promising them money . . . but they would not hearken to him but knocked him in head, and stripped him naked, and split open his bowels. Another, seeing many of the Indians about his barn, ventured and went out, but was quickly shot down. There were three others belonging to the same garrison who were killed; the Indians getting up upon the roof of the barn, had advantage to shoot down upon them over their fortification. Thus these murderous wretches went on, burning, and destroying before them. At length they came and beset our own house, and quickly it was the dolefulest day that ever mine eyes saw. The house stood upon the edge of a hill; some of the Indians got behind the hill, others into the barn, and others behind anything that could shelter them; from all which places they shot against the house, so that the bullets seemed to fly like hail; and quickly they wounded one man among us, then another, and then a third. About two hours . . . they had been about the house before they prevailed to fire it which they did with flax and hemp, which they brought out of the barn, and there being no defense about the house, only two flankers at two opposite corners and one of them not finished; they fired it once and one ventured out and quenched it, but they quickly fired it again, and that took. Now is the dreadful hour come, that I have often heard of in time of war, as it was the case of others, but now mine eyes see it. Some in our house were fighting for their lives, others wallowing in their blood, the house on fire over our heads, and the bloody heathen ready to knock us on the head, if we stirred out. Now might we hear mothers and children crying out for themselves, and one another, "Lord, what shall we do?" Then I took my children . . . to go forth and leave the house: but as soon as we came to the door and appeared, the Indians shot so thick that the bullets rattled against the house, as if one had taken an handful of stones and threw them, so that we were fain to give back. We had six stout dogs belonging to our garrison, but none of them would stir, though another time, if any Indian had come to the door, they were ready to fly upon him and tear him down. The Lord hereby would make us the more acknowledge His hand, and to see that our help is always in Him. But out we must go, the fire increasing, and coming along behind us, roaring, and the Indians gaping before us with their guns, spears, and hatchets to devour us . . . There were twelve killed, some shot, some stabbed with their spears, some knocked down with their hatchets . . . There was one who was chopped into the head with a hatchet, and stripped naked, and yet was crawling up and down. It is a solemn sight to see so many Christians lying in their blood, some here, and some there, like a company of sheep torn by wolves, all of them stripped naked by a company of hell-hounds, roaring, singing, ranting, and insulting, as if they would have torn our very hearts out; yet the Lord by His almighty power preserved a number of us from death, for there were twenty-four of us taken alive and carried captive.

Continues on next page

Lesson 4, Teacher's Guides for Bonus Battle

Marlborough Region: Battle of Lancaster, Continued

Possible Team Questions

- Q: What finally drove the speaker and her family out of the house? A: Fire

- Q: What town is under attack in this account? A: Lancaster

- Q: What kind of animals were unusually quiet? A: Dogs

- Q: What was one material the Indians used to set fire to the house? A: Flax and/or hemp

- Q: How many people were taken captive? A: 24

- Q: What did one wounded man promise the Indians for his life? A: Money

- Q: What high place did the Indians use to shoot from? A: The roof of the barn

- Q: To what religion does the speaker frequently refer? A: Christianity

Source: Mary Rowlandson: Narrative of the Captivity and Restoration of Mrs. Mary Rowlandson (1682)

Lesson 4, Teacher's Guides for Bonus Battle
Great Swamp Region:
The Great Swamp Battle

Great Swamp Fight: North American Colonial Wars

In the fall of 1675, King Philip's forces attacked and destroyed numerous colonial towns in southern New England. In short order his forces grew both in confidence and in numbers. The large and powerful Narragansett tribe, situated in Rhode Island, was officially neutral. However, colonial leaders believed that some Narragansett warriors were secretly joining King Philip's raiding parties and that the tribe itself was harboring wounded warriors. Determined to put an end to such assistance, the commissioners of the New England Confederation recalled most militia units from the western frontier. They also recruited new units, assembling the largest colonial force America had seen to that point. On December 9, 1675, a force that numbered more than 1,000 men marched from Massachusetts Bay toward the Rhode Island stronghold of the Narragansetts. The Narragansetts had decided to winter in a great fortification on the edges of the Great Swamp. The natives felt safe there in their nearly completed fortification, especially as they knew that the English disliked fighting in the thick woods and swampy land that surrounded the stronghold. On December 13, 1675, the majority of the colonial army gathered at Wickford, Rhode Island, on the outskirts of the Great Swamp. From there they spent several days attacking nearby native enclaves. The winter weather had made traversing the land easier for the militiamen, for it had stripped the leaves from the underbrush and frozen the otherwise swampy ground. In one of these attacks, the colonists captured a warrior named Indian Peter, who promised to lead them to the Narragansett fort. On December 18, the colonial forces moved into the swamp, led by Indian Peter. They sighted their objective the next afternoon. The fort was constructed of wooden palisades with a mass of brush and timber around the base of the wall and small blockhouses at each corner. A sizable village of huts lay within the walls. At the time of the colonial attack, there were some 1,000 natives in the fort. Without time to properly plan an attack, the vanguard of the colonial army rushed the fort. With incredible luck, they happened upon a gap in the wall, although it was protected by a nearby blockhouse. Two companies rushed the opening and broke through, only to lose their captains and be forced back. As other troops rushed forward, they were able to break into the village and forced the Narragansetts to fall back. The fight inside became a series of individual battles among the Indian dwellings. The colonial leader Captain Winslow, worried about the fierce fighting, gave the order to burn the fort to force the natives into the open. Winslow's aide, Captain Benjamin Church, tried to dissuade him, arguing that the colonials might use the fort for shelter after the battle was won. However, the militiamen began to burn the huts, with men, women, and children still inside. It was a scene reminiscent of the English attack on the Mystic Fort during the Pequot War. Soon, the entire fort was on fire. While some warriors escaped into the woods, many more natives, mostly women, children, and the elderly, died in the fire. Contemporary estimates of Native

Continues on next page

Lesson 4, Teacher's Guides for Bonus Battle

Great Swamp Region: The Great Swamp Battle, Continued

American dead range from 600 to as many as 1,000. The colonials lost 20 immediately killed and some 200 wounded. Within a month, the toll of the colonial dead had risen to 70 to 80. Losses were especially high among the officers. While the campaign was considered a success, this came at a heavy price. The Narragansett Indians, previously neutral, now openly joined King Philip's warriors.

Possible Team Questions

- Q: How many English soldiers fought in this battle? A: 1,000

- Q: What region is under attack in this account? A: The Great Swamp

- Q: What type of English soldiers suffered the greatest losses? A: The officers

- Q: Why was the swamp not as troublesome as it might have been? A: The ground was frozen

- Q: How did the English ultimately defeat the Indians? A: They burned the fort

- Q: Estimate the number of Indians killed. A: 600–1,000

- Q: What was the "high price" paid for this victory? A: The Narragansetts joined King Philip

- Q: The author compares this battle to another already studied. Which one? A: Mystic Fort

Source: Zelner, Kyle F. "Great Swamp Fight: North American Colonial Wars." Available at *United States at War: Understanding Conflict and Society.* 2008. ABC-CLIO. 14 Mar. 2008 *http://www.usatwar.abc-clio.com*

Teacher's Guides for Bonus Battle
Deerfield Region: Bloody Brook Massacre

In mid-September 1675, as fighting along Massachusetts Bay's western frontier worsened during King Philip's War (1675–1676), colonial officials decided to abandon a number of outlying towns and consolidate their defenses. Deerfield, Massachusetts, was one of the towns abandoned, but its grain warehouses and barns were full of drying corn—food that would be greatly needed that winter. In mid-September 1675, Captain Thomas Lathrop was ordered to protect the wagon caravan carrying the corn from Deerfield south to Springfield. Lathrop and his Essex County militia company of some 60 to 70 men prepared themselves for the task at hand. They loaded the carts the night of September 18. The next morning, September 19, Lathrop and his company, as well as the local teamsters in charge of the carts, set off. Captain Samuel Mosley's militia company scouted the area ahead of the wagon train. Lathrop reportedly was confident that no Indian party would attack such a large military force. He held that the Native American war parties struck only defenseless garrison houses and isolated farms. Accordingly, Lathrop had not positioned flankers or a vanguard. The wagon train traveled south along the forest path. When they reached Muddy Brook, about five miles south of Deerfield, Lathrop and his men found themselves quickly surrounded by hundreds of Wampanoags, Pocumtucks, Nipmucks, and other Native Americans. The Indians attacked with deadly speed and efficiency. Ever after Muddy Brook was known as Bloody Brook. In his history of the war, Increase Mather claimed that Lathrop's men were so confident and carefree that they had placed their muskets in the carts in order to eat wild grapes along the stream bank, rendering them defenseless. The ambush was over in just a few minutes. At least 60 colonials were slain, including Captain Lathrop and 15 of the Deerfield men. Hearing the frantic calls of Lathrop's bugler, who had escaped the carnage, Captain Mosley and his company hurried to the scene, rushing the Indians and scattering the scalp hunters. As Mosley's scouting unit and the few survivors from the ambush struggled back to Deerfield that evening, they were taunted by Indians in the distance, who held aloft as trophies clothing from Lathrop's men's bodies. The next day, Mosley and his men returned to Bloody Creek to bury the English dead, including Captain Lathrop. When news of the ambush or massacre traveled east, especially Essex County, the entire colony went into mourning. Rev. William Hubbard called it "that most fatal day, the saddest day that ever befel New England . . . the Ruine of a choice Company of young men, the very Flower of Essex." The Bloody Brook Massacre is only one example from among hundreds of the style of wilderness warfare known as the "skulking way of war." Native Americans had long practiced the tactic of ambush, and their adoption of European firearms only made it more deadly. While colonial militias throughout the colonies were at first almost always the victims of ambush and other types of irregular warfare, some militia commanders adopted Indian tactics and eventually gave as good as they got.

Continues on next page

Teacher's Guide for Bonus Battle

Deerfield Region: Bloody Brook Massacre, Continued

Possible Team Questions

- Q: What was the name of the town that had been abandoned? A: Deerfield

- Q: What was Captain Thomas Lathrop specifically guarding? A: Wagon caravan of corn

- Q: What was the real name for the creek they were crossing? A: Muddy Brook

- Q: What had the overconfident soldiers done to make themselves defenseless? A: Put their guns in the wagons so they could eat grapes

- Q: How did Captain Mosley know there was a battle going on? A: He heard the bugler.

- Q: What was the phrase for this ambush style of Indian attack? A: "Skulking" or "skulking way of war"

- Q: How did English commanders change their style of warfare tactics? A: They adopted similar ambush after battles like this one.

Source: Zelner, Kyle F. "Battle of Bloody Brook" in *The Encyclopedia of North American Colonial Conflicts to 1775: A Political, Social, and Military History.* Edited by Spencer C. Tucker. Santa Barbara, CA: ABC-CLIO, 2008.

King Philip and New England Colonial Expansion in the 1670s

Lesson 1, Illustration
Scenes from the Pequot War

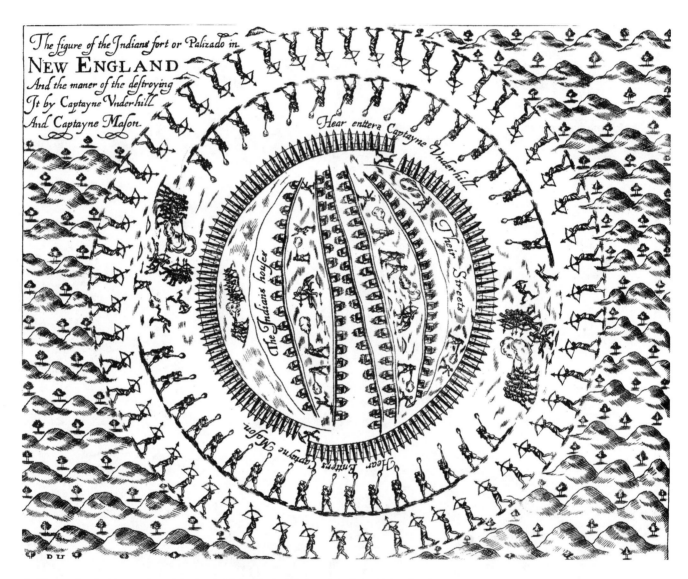

▲ Illustration in *Newes from America* by John Underhill. London: Printed by J.D. for Peter Cole, [...], 1638. (Library of Congress)

Lesson 2, Excerpts for Individual Student Work
King Philip's War, Report by Edward Randolph

1. *"Various are the reports of the causes of the present Indian warre. Some impute it to an imprudent zeal in the magistrates of Boston to Christianize those heathen before they were civilized."*

2. *"Enjoining them the strict observation of their laws, which, to a people so rude and licentious, hath proved even intolerable."*

3. *"The people entice and provoke the Indians especially to drunkenness, to which those people are so generally addicted, they will strip themselves to their skin to have their fill of rum and brandy."*

4. *"the Massachusetts having made a law that every Indian drunk should pay 10s. or be whipped, according to the discretion of the magistrate. Many of these poor people willingly offered their backs to the lash to save their money."*

5. *"the magistrates finding much trouble and no profit to arise to the government by whipping, did change that punishment into 10 days work. For such as could not or would not pay the fine which did highly incense the Indians."*

6. *"Some believe there have been priests, who have made it their business to go from Sachem to Sachem, to exasperate the Indians against the English and to bring them into a confederacy."*

7. *"They were promised supplies from France and other parts to extirpate the English nation out of the continent of America."*

Continues on next page

Lesson 2, Excerpts for Individual Student Work

King Philip's War, Report by Edward Randolph, Continued

8. *"Others impute the cause to some injuries offered to the Sachem Philip; He being possessed of a tract of land called Mount Hope some English had a mind to dispossess him thereof, who complained of injuries done by Philip and his Indians to their stock and cattle."*

9. *"Philip was often summoned before the magistrate and never released but upon parting with a considerable part of his land."*

10. *"The government of Massachusetts does declare these are the great evils for which God hath given the heathen commission to rise against them."*

11. *The woeful breach of the 5th commandment, in contempt of their authority, which is a sin highly provoking to the Lord.*

12. *"For men wearing long hair and periwigs made of women's hair; for women . . . cutting, curling and laying out the hair, for women wearing borders of hair and for cutting, curling and laying out the hair, and disguising themselves by following strange fashions in their apparel.*

13. *For profaneness in the people not frequenting their meetings, and others going away before the blessing be pronounced.*

14. *For suffering the Quakers to live amongst them and to set up their thresholds by God's thresholds, contrary to their old laws and resolutions.*

Lesson 2, Excerpts for Individual Student Work

King Philip's War, Report by Edward Randolph, Continued

15. *"With many such reasons, but whatever be the cause, the English have contributed much to their misfortunes."*

16. *"For they first taught the Indians the use of arms, and admitted them to be present at all their musters and trainings, shewed them how to handle, mend and fix their muskets."*

17. *"Have been furnished with all sorts of arms by permission of the government so that the Indians are become excellent firemen."*

18. *"And at Natick there was a gathered church of praying Indians, who were exercised as trained bands, under officers of their own."*

19. *"these have been the most barbarous and cruel enemies to the English of any others. Capt. Tom, their leader, being lately taken and hanged at Boston, with one other of their chiefs."*

20. *"That notwithstanding, the ancient law of the country, made in the year 1633, that no person should sell any arms or ammunition to any Indian upon penalty of £10 for every gun, £5 for a pound of powder, and 40s. for a pound of shot."*

21. *"giving liberty to all such as should have license from them to sell, unto any Indian, guns, swords, powder and shot, paying to the treasurer 3d. for each gun and for each dozen of swords; 6d. for a pound of powder and for every ten pounds of shot."*

Continues on next page

Lesson 2, Excerpts for Individual Student Work

King Philip's War, Report by Edward Randolph, Continued

22. *"by which means the Indians have been abundantly furnished with great store of arms and ammunition to the utter ruin and undoing of many families in the neighboring colonies to enrich some few of their relations and church members."*

23. *"No advantage but many disadvantages have arisen to the English by the war, for about 600 men have been slain, and 12 captains, most of them brave and stout persons and of loyal principles, whilst the church members had liberty to stay at home and not hazard their persons in the wilderness."*

24. *"The loss to the English in the several colonies, in their habitations and stock, is reckoned to amount to £150,000 there having been about 1200 houses burned, 8000 head of cattle, great and small, killed, and many thousand bushels of wheat, peas and other grain burned."*

25. *"upward of 3000 Indians men women and children destroyed, who if well managed would have been very serviceable to the English, which makes all manner of labor dear."*

26. *"The war at present is near an end. In Plymouth colony the Indians surrender themselves to Gov. Winslow, upon mercy, and bring in all their arms, are wholly at his disposal, except life and transportation;"*

27. *"but for all such as have been notoriously cruel to women and children, so soon as discovered they are to be executed in the sight of their fellow Indians."*

Lesson 2, Excerpts, for Small Group Work
Excerpt 1, *King Philip's War,* Report by Edward Randolph

Various are the reports and conjectures of the causes of the present Indian war. Some impute it to an imprudent zeal in the magistrates of Boston to Christianize those heathen before they were civilized and enjoining them the strict observation of their laws, which, to a people so rude and licentious, hath proved even intolerable, and that the more, for that while the magistrates, for their profit, put the laws severely in execution against the Indians, the people, on the other side, for lucre and gain, entice and provoke the Indians to the breach thereof, especially to drunkenness, to which those people are so generally addicted that they will strip themselves to their skin to have their fill of rum and brandy, the Massachusetts having made a law that every Indian drunk should pay 10s. or be whipped, according to the discretion of the magistrate. Many of these poor people willingly offered their backs to the lash to save their money; whereupon, the magistrates finding much trouble and no profit to arise to the government by whipping, did change that punishment into 10 days work for such as could not or would not pay the fine of 10 shillings which did highly incense the Indians.

Lesson 2, Excerpts, for Small Group Work
Excerpt 2, *King Philip's War,* Report by Edward Randolph

Some believe there have been vagrant and Jesuitical priests, who have made it their business, for some years past, to go from Sachem to Sachem, to exasperate the Indians against the English and to bring them into a confederacy, and that they were promised supplies from France and other parts to extirpate the English nation out of the continent of America. Others impute the cause to some injuries offered to the Sachem Philip; for he being possessed of a tract of land called Mount Hope, a very fertile, pleasant and rich soil, some English had a mind to dispossess him thereof, who never wanting one pretence or other to attain their end, complained of injuries done by Philip and his Indians to their stock and cattle, whereupon Philip was often summoned before the magistrate, sometimes imprisoned, and never released but upon parting with a considerable part of his land.

Lesson 2, Excerpts for Small Group Work
Excerpt 3, *King Philip's War,* Report by Edward Randolph

But the government of the Massachusetts (to give it in their own words) do declare these are the great evils for which God hath given the heathen commission to rise against them: The woeful breach of the 5th commandment, in contempt of their authority, which is a sin highly provoking to the Lord: For men wearing long hair and perewigs made of women's hair; for women wearing borders of hair and for cutting, curling and laying out the hair, and disguising themselves by following strange fashions in their apparel: For profaneness in the people not frequenting their meetings, and others going away before the blessing be pronounced: For suffering the Quakers to live amongst them and to set up their thresholds by Gods thresholds, contrary to their old laws and resolutions.

Lesson 2, Excerpts for Small Group Work
Excerpt 4, *King Philip's War,* Report by Edward Randolph

With many such reasons, but whatever be the cause, the English have contributed much to their misfortunes, for they first taught the Indians the use of arms, and admitted them to be present at all their musters and trainings, and shewed them how to handle, mend and fix their muskets, and have been furnished with all sorts of arms by permission of the government, so that the Indians are become excellent firemen. And at Natick there was a gathered church of praying Indians, who were exercised as trained bands, under officers of their own; these have been the most barbarous and cruel enemies to the English of any others. Capt. Tom, their leader, being lately taken and hanged at Boston, with one other of their chiefs.

Lesson 2, Excerpts, for Small Group Work

Excerpt 5, *King Philip's War*, Report by Edward Randolph

That notwithstanding the ancient law of the country, made in the year 1633, that no person should sell any arms or ammunition to any Indian upon penalty of £10 for every gun, £5 for a pound of powder, and 40s. for a pound of shot, yet the government of the Massachusetts in the year 1657, upon design to monopolize the whole Indian trade did publish and declare that the trade of furs and peltry with the Indians in their jurisdiction did solely and properly belong to their commonwealth and not to every indifferent person, and did enact that no person should trade with the Indians for any sort of peltry, except such as were authorized by that court, under the penalty of £100 for every offence, giving liberty to all such as should have license from them to sell, unto any Indian, guns, swords, powder and shot, paying to the treasurer 3d. for each gun and for each dozen of swords; 6d. for a pound of powder and for every ten pounds of shot, by which means the Indians have been abundantly furnished with great store of arms and ammunition to the utter ruin and undoing of many families in the neighboring colonies to enrich some few of their relations and church members.

Lesson 2, Excerpts for Small Group Work

Excerpt 6, *King Philip's War*, Report by Edward Randolph

No advantage but many disadvantages have arisen to the English by the war, for about 600 men have been slain, and 12 captains, most of them brave and stout persons and of loyal principles, whilst the church members had liberty to stay at home and not hazard their persons in the wilderness. The loss to the English in the several colonies, in their habitations and stock, is reckoned to amount to £150,000 there having been about 1200 houses burned, 8000 head of cattle, great and small, killed, and many thousand bushels of wheat, peas and other grain burned (of which the Massachusetts colony hath not been damnifyed one third part, the great loss falling upon New Plymouth and Connecticut colonies) and upward of 3000 Indians men women and children destroyed, who if well managed would have been very serviceable to the English, which makes all manner of labor dear. The war at present is near an end. In Plymouth colony the Indians surrender themselves to Gov. Winslow, upon mercy, and bring in all their arms, are wholly at his disposal, except life and transportation; but for all such as have been notoriously cruel to women and children, so soon as discovered they are to be executed in the sight of their fellow Indians.

Lesson 2, Excerpt for Whole Class Activity
A Relation of the Indian War, by John Easton

King Philip's Words as Retold by John Easton, Attorney General of Rhode Island

(This primary source has been abridged for spelling)

They said they had been the first in doing good to the English, and the English the first in doing wrong; They said when the English first came, their King's Father was as a great man, and the English as a little child; he constrained other Indians from wronging the English, and gave them corn and showed them how to plant, and was free to do them any good, and had let them have a 100 times more land than now the King had for his own people. But their King's Brother, [Massasoit] when he was King, came miserably to die by being forced to court, as they judge poisoned. And another grievance was, if 20 of their honest Indians testified that a Englishman had done them wrong, it was as nothing; and if but one of their worst Indians testified against any Indian or their King, when it pleased the English, it was sufficient. Another Grievance was, when their king sold land, the English would say, it was more than they agreed to, and a writing must be prove against all them, and some of their kings had done wrong to sell so much. He left his people none, And some being given to drunkenness the English made them drunk and then cheated them in bargains, but now their kings were forewarned not for to part with land, for nothing in comparison to the value thereof. Now home the English had owned for King or Queen, they would disinherit, and make another King that would give or sell them these Lands; that now, they had no hopes left to keep any land. Another Grievance, the English cattle and horses still increased; that when they removed 30 Miles from where English had any thing to do, they could not keep their corn from being spoiled, they never being used to fence, and thought when the English bought land of them they would have kept their cattle upon their own land. Another grievance, the English were so eager to sell the Indians liquors, that most of the Indians spent all in drunkenness, and then ravened upon the sober Indians, and they did believe often did hurt the English cattle, and their King could not prevent it. We knew before, these were their grand complaints, but then we only endeavored to persuade that all complaints might be righted without war, but could have no other answer but that they had not heard of that way for the Governor of York and an Indian King to have the hearing of it. We had cause to think in that had been tendered it would have been accepted. We endeavored that however they should lay down the war, for the English were too strong for them; they said, then the English should do to them as they did when they were too strong for the English.

—Easton, John, *A Relation of the Indian War, by Mr. Easton, of Rhode Island*, 1675

Lesson 3, Excerpts from Mary Rowlandson's Journal
Excerpt 1

Though I saw them not, they presently called me in, and bade me sit down and not stir. Then they catched up their guns, and away they ran, as if an enemy had been at hand, and the guns went off apace. I manifested some great trouble, and they asked me what was the matter? I told them I thought they had killed the English-man (for they had in the meantime informed me that an Englishman was come). They said, no. They shot over his horse and under and before his horse, and they pushed him this way and that way, at their pleasure, showing what they could do . . . When they had talked their fill with him, they suffered me to go to him. We asked each other of our welfare, and how my husband did, and all my friends? He told me they were all well, and would be glad to see me. Amongst other things which my husband sent me, there came a pound of tobacco, which I sold for nine shillings in money; for many of the Indians for want of tobacco, smoked hemlock, and ground ivy. It was a great mistake in any, who thought I sent for tobacco; for through the favor of God, that desire was overcome.

A

NARRATIVE

OF THE

Captivity, Sufferings, and Removes,

OF

Mrs. Mary Rowlandfon,

Who was taken Prisoner by the Indians; with several others;
and treated in the moft barbarous and cruel Manner by the
wild Savages: With many other remarkable Events during her Travels.

*Written by her own Hand, for her private Use, and since
made public at the earnest Desire of some Friends, and for
the Benefit of the Afflicted.*

Lesson 3, Excerpts from Mary Rowlandson's Journal
Excerpt 2

At night we came to an Indian town, and the Indians sat down by a wigwam dis-coursing, but I was almost spent, and could scarce speak. I laid down my load, and went into the wigwam, and there sat an Indian boiling of horses feet (they being wont to eat the flesh first, and when the feet were old and dried, and they had noth-ing else, they would cut off the feet and use them). I asked him to give me a little of his broth, or water they were boiling in; he took a dish, and gave me one spoonful of samp, and bid me take as much of the broth as I would. Then I put some of the hot water to the samp, and drank it up, and my spirit came again. He gave me also a piece of the ruff or ridding of the small guts, and I broiled it on the coals.

Lesson 3, Excerpts from Mary Rowlandson's Journal
Excerpt 3

A

NARRATIVE

OF THE

Captivity, Sufferings, and Removes,

OF

Mrs. Mary Rowlandſon,

Who was taken Priſoner by the Indians; with ſeveral others;
and treated in the moſt barbarous and cruel Manner by the
wild Savages: With many other remarkable Events during her Travels.

Written by her own Hand, for her private Uſe, and ſince
made public at the earneſt Deſire of ſome Friends, and for
the Benefit of the Afflicted.

We traveled on till night; and in the morning, we must go over the river to Philip's crew. When I was in the canoe I could not but be amazed at the numerous crew of pagans that were on the bank on the other side. When I came ashore, they gathered all about me, I sitting alone in the midst. I observed they asked one another questions, and laughed, and rejoiced over their gains and victories. Then my heart began to fail: and I fell aweeping, which was the first time to my remembrance, that I wept before them . . . There one of them asked me why I wept. I could hardly tell what to say: Yet I answered, they would kill me. "No," said he, "none will hurt you." Then came one of them and gave me two spoonfuls of meal to comfort me, and another gave me half a pint of peas.

Lesson 3, Excerpts from Mary Rowlandson's Journal
Excerpt 4

I went to see King Philip. He bade me come in and sit down, and asked me whether I would smoke it (a usual compliment nowadays amongst saints and sinners) but this no way suited me. For though I had formerly used tobacco, yet I had left it ever since I was first taken. It seems to be a bait the devil lays to make men lose their precious time. I remember with shame how formerly, when I had taken two or three pipes, I was presently ready for another, such a bewitching thing it is. But I thank God, He has now given me power over it; surely there are many who may be better employed than to lie sucking a stinking tobacco-pipe. Now the Indians gather their forces to go against Northampton. Over night one went about yelling and hooting to give notice of the design. Whereupon they fell to boiling of ground nuts, and parching of corn (as many as had it) for their provision; and in the morning away they went.

Lesson 3, Excerpts from Mary Rowlandson's Journal
Excerpt 5

It was upon a Sabbath-day-morning, that they prepared for their travel. This morning I asked my master whether he would sell me to my husband. He answered me "Nux," which did much rejoice my spirit. My mistress, before we went, was gone to the burial of a papoose, and returning, she found me sitting and reading in my Bible; she snatched it hastily out of my hand, and threw it out of doors. I ran out and catched it up, and put it into my pocket, and never let her see it afterward. Then they packed up their things to be gone, and gave me my load. I complained it was too heavy, whereupon she gave me a slap in the face, and bade me go; I lifted up my heart to God, hoping the redemption was not far off; and the rather because their insolency grew worse and worse.

A
NARRATIVE
OF THE
Captivity, Sufferings, and Removes,
OF
Mrs. Mary Rowlandson,
Who was taken Prisoner by the Indians; with several others; and treated in the moſt barbarous and cruel Manner by the wild Savages: With many other remarkable Events during her Travels.
Written by her own Hand, for her private Uſe, and since made public at the earnest Desire of some Friends, and for the Benefit of the Afflicted.

Lesson 3, Excerpts from Mary Rowlandson's Journal
Excerpt 6

Hearing that my son was come to this place, I went to see him, and found him lying flat upon the ground. I asked him how he could sleep so? He answered me that he was not asleep, but at prayer; and lay so, that they might not observe what he was doing. I pray God he may remember these things now he is returned in safety. There was here one Mary Thurston of Medfield, who seeing how it was with me, lent me a hat to wear; but as soon as I was gone, the squaw (who owned that Mary Thurston) came running after me, and got it away again. Here was the squaw that gave me one spoonful of meal. I put it in my pocket to keep it safe. Yet notwithstanding, somebody stole it, but put five Indian corns in the room of it; which corns were the greatest provisions I had in my travel for one day.

Lesson 3, Excerpts from Mary Rowlandson's Journal
Excerpt 7

During my abode in this place, Philip spake to me to make a shirt for his boy, which I did, for which he gave me a shilling. I offered the money to my master, but he bade me keep it; and with it I bought a piece of horse flesh. Afterwards he asked me to make a cap for his boy, for which he invited me to dinner. I went, and he gave me a pancake, about as big as two fingers. It was made of parched wheat, beaten, and fried in bear's grease, but I thought I never tasted pleasanter meat in my life. There was a squaw who spake to me to make a shirt for her sannup, for which she gave me a piece of bear. Another asked me to knit a pair of stockings, for which she gave me a quart of peas.

Lesson 3, Excerpts from Mary Rowlandson's Journal
Excerpt 8

Amongst them also was that poor woman before mentioned, who came to a sad end, as some of the company told me in my travel: she having much grief upon her spirit about her miserable condition, being so near her time, she would be often asking the Indians to let her go home; they not being willing to that, and yet vexed with her importunity, gathered a great company together about her and stripped her naked, and set her in the midst of them, and when they had sung and danced about her (in their hellish manner) as long as they pleased they knocked her on head, and the child in her arms with her. When they had done that they made a fire and put them both into it, and told the other children that were with them that if they attempted to go home, they would serve them in like manner. The children said she did not shed one tear, but prayed all the while.

Lesson 3, Excerpts from Mary Rowlandson's Journal
Excerpt 9

My master had three squaws, living sometimes with one, and sometimes with another one, this old squaw, at whose wigwam I was, and with whom my master had been those three weeks. Another was Weetamoo with whom I had lived and served all this while. A severe and proud dame she was, bestowing every day in dressing herself neat as much time as any of the gentry of the land: powdering her hair, and painting her face, going with necklaces, with jewels in her ears, and bracelets upon her hands. When she had dressed herself, her work was to make girdles of wampum and beads. The third squaw was a younger one, by whom he had two papooses. By the time I was refreshed by the old squaw, with whom my master was, Weetamoo's maid came to call me home, at which I fell aweeping. Then the old squaw told me, to encourage me, that if I wanted victuals, I should come to her, and that I should lie there in her wigwam. Then I went with the maid, and quickly came again and lodged there. The squaw laid a mat under me, and a good rug over me; the first time I had any such kindness showed me.

A

NARRATIVE

OF THE

Captivity, Sufferings, and Removes,

OF

Mrs. Mary Rowlandſon,

Who was taken Prisoner by the Indians; with several others; and treated in the moſt barbarous and cruel Manner by the wild Savages: With many other remarkable Events during her Travels.

Written by her own Hand, for her private Uſe, and since made public at the earneſt Desire of some Friends, and for the Benefit of the Afflicted.

Lesson 3, Excerpts from Mary Rowlandson's Journal
Excerpt 10

When my master came home, he came to me and bid me make a shirt for his papoose, of a holland-laced pillowbere. About that time there came an Indian to me and bid me come to his wigwam at night, and he would give me some pork and ground nuts. Which I did, and as I was eating, another Indian said to me, he seems to be your good friend, but he killed two Englishmen at Sudbury, and there lie their clothes behind you: I looked behind me, and there I saw bloody clothes, with bullet-holes in them. Yet the Lord suffered not this wretch to do me any hurt. Yea, instead of that, he many times refreshed me; five or six times did he and his squaw refresh my feeble carcass. If I went to their wigwam at any time, they would always give me something, and yet they were strangers that I never saw before. Another squaw gave me a piece of fresh pork, and a little salt with it, and lent me her pan to fry it in; and I cannot but remember what a sweet, pleasant and delightful relish that bit had to me, to this day. So little do we prize common mercies when we have them to the full.

Lesson 3, Excerpts from Mary Rowlandson's Journal
Excerpt 11

Before they went to that fight they got a company together to pow-wow . . . There was one that kneeled upon a deerskin, with the company round him in a ring who kneeled, and striking upon the ground with their hands, and with sticks, and muttering or humming with their mouths. Besides him who kneeled in the ring, there also stood one with a gun in his hand. Then he on the deerskin made a speech, and all manifested assent to it; and so they did many times together. Then they bade him with the gun go out of the ring, which he did. But when he was out, they called him in again; but he seemed to make a stand; then they called the more earnestly, till he returned again. Then they all sang. Then they gave him two guns, in either hand one. And so he on the deerskin began again; and at the end of every sentence in his speaking, they all assented, humming or muttering with their mouths, and striking upon the ground with their hands. Then they bade him with the two guns go out of the ring again; which he did, a little way. Then they called him in again, but he made a stand. So they called him with greater earnestness; but he stood reeling and wavering as if he knew not whither he should stand or fall, or which way to go. Then they called him with exceeding great vehemency, all of them, one and another. After a little while he turned in, staggering as he went, with his arms stretched out, in either hand a gun. As soon as he came in they all sang and rejoiced exceedingly a while.

A

NARRATIVE

OF THE

Captivity, Sufferings, and Removes,

OF

Mrs. Mary Rowlandſon,

Who was taken Prisoner by the Indians; with several others; and treated in the moſt barbarous and cruel Manner by the wild Savages: With many other remarkable Events during her Travels.

Written by her own Hand, for her private Uſe, and since made public at the earneſt Desire of some Friends, and for the Benefit of the Afflicted.

Lesson 3, Excerpts from Mary Rowlandson's Journal
Excerpt 12

Mr. Hoar called them betime to dinner, but they ate very little, they being so busy in dressing themselves, and getting ready for their dance, which was carried on by eight of them, four men and four squaws. My master and mistress being two. He was dressed in his holland shirt, with great laces sewed at the tail of it; he had his silver buttons, his white stockings, his garters were hung round with shillings, and he had girdles of wampum upon his head and shoulders. She had a kersey coat, and covered with girdles of wampum from the loins upward. Her arms from her elbows to her hands were covered with bracelets; there were handfuls of necklaces about her neck, and several sorts of jewels in her ears. She had fine red stockings, and white shoes, her hair powdered and face painted red, that was always before black. And all the dancers were after the same manner. There were two others singing and knocking on a kettle for their music. They kept hopping up and down one after another, with a kettle of water in the midst, standing warm upon some embers, to drink of when they were dry. They held on till it was almost night, throwing out wampum to the standers by.

Lesson 3, Excerpts from Mary Rowlandson's Journal
Excerpt 13

Strangely did the Lord provide for them; that I did not see (all the time I was among them) one man, woman, or child, die with hunger. Though many times they would eat that, that a hog or a dog would hardly touch; yet by that God strengthened them to be a scourge to His people. The chief and commonest food was ground nuts. They eat also nuts and acorns, artichokes, lilly roots, ground beans, and several other weeds and roots, that I know not. They would pick up old bones, and cut them to pieces at the joints, and if they were full of worms and maggots, they would scald them over the fire to make the vermine come out, and then boil them, and drink up the liquor, and then beat the great ends of them in a mortar, and so eat them. They would eat horse's guts, and ears, and all sorts of wild birds which they could catch; also bear, venison, beaver, tortoise, frogs, squirrels, dogs, skunks, rattlesnakes; yea, the very bark of trees; besides all sorts of creatures, and provision which they plundered from the English. I can but stand in admiration to see the wonderful power of God in providing for such a vast number of our enemies in the wilderness.

A

NARRATIVE

OF THE

Captivity, Sufferings, and Removes,

OF

Mrs. Mary Rowlandſon,

Who was taken Prisoner by the Indians ; with several others ; and treated in the moſt barbarous and cruel Manner by the wild Savages : With many other remarkable Events during her Travels.

Written by her own Hand, for her private Use, and since made public at the earnest Desire of some Friends, and for the Benefit of the Afflicted.

DEFINING MOMENT I

Lesson 3, Excerpts from Mary Rowlandson's Journal
Excerpt 14

Towards night I gathered some sticks for my own comfort, that I might not lie a-cold; but when we came to lie down they bade me to go out, and lie somewhere else, for they had company (they said) come in more than their own. I told them, I could not tell where to go, they bade me go look; I told them, if I went to another wigwam they would be angry, and send me home again. Then one of the company drew his sword, and told me he would run me through if I did not go presently. Then was I fain to stoop to this rude fellow, and to go out in the night, I knew not whither . . . I went to one wigwam, and they told me they had no room. Then I went to another, and they said the same; at last an old Indian bade me to come to him, and his squaw gave me some ground nuts; she gave me also something to lay under my head, and a good fire we had; and through the good providence of God, I had a comfortable lodging that night.

Lesson 3, Excerpts from Mary Rowlandson's Journal
Excerpt 15

On the Saturday they boiled an old horse's leg which they had got, and so we drank of the broth, as soon as they thought it was ready, and when it was almost all gone, they filled it up again. The first week of my being among them I hardly ate any thing; the second week I found my stomach grow very faint for want of something; and yet it was very hard to get down their filthy trash; but the third week, though I could think how formerly my stomach would turn against this or that, and I could starve and die before I could eat such things, yet they were sweet and savory to my taste. I was at this time knitting a pair of white cotton stockings for my mistress; and had not yet wrought upon a Sabbath day. When the Sabbath came they bade me go to work. I told them it was the Sabbath day, and desired them to let me rest, and told them I would do as much more tomorrow; to which they answered me they would break my face. And here I cannot but take notice of the strange providence of God in preserving the heathen. They were many hundreds, old and young, some sick, and some lame; many had papooses at their backs. The greatest number at this time with us were squaws, and they traveled with all they had, bag and baggage, and yet they got over this river aforesaid; and on Monday they set their wigwams on fire, and away they went.

A

NARRATIVE

OF THE

Captivity, Sufferings, and Removes,

OF

Mrs. Mary Rowlandſon,

Who was taken Priſoner by the Indians; with ſeveral others; and treated in the moſt barbarous and cruel Manner by the wild Savages: With many other remarkable Events during her Travels.

Written by her own Hand, for her private Uſe, and ſince made public at the earneſt Deſire of ſome Friends, and for the Benefit of the Afflicted.

Lesson 3, Excerpts from Mary Rowlandson's Journal
Excerpt 16

A

NARRATIVE

OF THE

Captivity, Sufferings, and Removes,

OF

Mrs. Mary Rowlandfon,

Who was taken Prisoner by the Indians; with several others; and treated in the moft barbarous and cruel Manner by the wild Savages: With many other remarkable Events during her Travels.

Written by her own Hand, for her private Use, and since made public at the earnest Desire of some Friends, and for the Benefit of the Afflicted.

That day, a little after noon, we came to Squakeag, where the Indians quickly spread themselves over the deserted English fields, gleaning what they could find. Some picked up ears of wheat that were crickled down; some found ears of Indian corn; some found ground nuts, and others sheaves of wheat that were frozen together in the shock, and went to threshing of them out. Myself got two ears of Indian corn, and whilst I did but turn my back, one of them was stolen from me, which much troubled me. There came an Indian to them at that time with a basket of horse liver. I asked him to give me a piece. "What," says he, "can you eat horse liver?" I told him, I would try, if he would give a piece, which he did, and I laid it on the coals to roast. But before it was half ready they got half of it away from me, so that I was fain to take the rest and eat it as it was, with the blood about my mouth, and yet a savory bit it was to me.

Lesson 3, Excerpts from Mary Rowlandson's Journal
Excerpt 17

In my travels an Indian came to me and told me, if I were willing, he and his squaw would run away, and go home along with me. I told him no: I was not willing to run away, but desired to wait God's time, that I might go home quietly, and without fear. And now God hath granted me my desire. O the wonderful power of God that I have seen, and the experience that I have had. I have been in the midst of those roaring lions, and savage bears, that feared neither God, nor man, nor the devil, by night and day, alone and in company, sleeping all sorts together, and yet not one of them ever offered me the least abuse of unchastity to me, in word or action. Though some are ready to say I speak it for my own credit; but I speak it in the presence of God, and to His Glory. God's power is as great now, and as sufficient to save, as when He preserved Daniel in the lion's den[.]

King Philip and New England Colonial Expansion in the 1670s

Glossary Terms

blockhouse

A blockhouse was a crude frontier fortification commonly used during the 17th and 18th centuries. Block-houses were typically two-story square or rectangular buildings made of logs or thick planks and topped with a sloping roof. Often, the second story overhung the first story to allow defenders to fire down on attackers. Many blockhouses were built by frontier communities to act as temporary refuges in case of attacks by Native Americans. Other blockhouses served as permanent strategic defensive works, and some were incorporated as part of a larger system of fortifications.

captivity narratives

Captivity narratives were accounts of white colonists who were kidnapped by, lived among, and either escaped from or were freed by Native Americans. Captivity narratives were an extremely popular literary genre during the colonial period. These frequently sensationalized stories often had a moralistic quality and helped to perpet-uate prejudice against Native Americans and the French, who were believed to be instigating these attacks. Famous captivity narratives include accounts by Alvar Núñez, Mary Rowlandson, and John Williams. The influ-ential Puritan Increase Mather did much to popularize captivity narratives in colonial North America.

Great Swamp Fortress

The Great Swamp Fortress was a redoubt constructed by the Narragansett Indians in the late 17th century in the so-called Great Swamp, located near present-day South Kingstown, Rhode Island. The Great Swamp Fortress, also known as Canochet's Fort, was built of earth reinforced by high palisades of fallen trees and was surrounded by a moat. The fortification served as the Narragansetts' winter encampment and was built deep in the swamp, making it difficult to approach or leave the redoubt. During King Philip's War, the fortress was the site of the Great Swamp Fight, during which New England militiamen attacked and set fire to the building, killing between 400 and 700 men, women, and children.

praying towns

Segregated communities created by the Puritans where Native American converts, known as praying Indians, were immersed in the English way of life while learning the tenets of Christianity. Based on a similar system used in New France, the first New England praying towns were devised by missionaries John Eliot and Daniel

Gookin. These communities were strictly governed, and inhabitants were usually not allowed to leave. The colonists hoped the praying Indians would serve as a buffer between colonial settlements and hostile Native American groups and would warn colonists of impending attacks. This rarely happened, however. Praying towns were never very popular, and by the time of King Philip's War there were only approximately 1,100 Native Americans living in 14 praying towns.

sachem

A term used to describe the leaders of certain northeastern Native American groups. Unlike the position of chief, which was based on personal merit or skill, the position of sachem was an inherited civil title. Sachems—who were usually but not always men—were responsible for such important tasks as distributing land, collecting tribute, receiving guests, and, occasionally, directing the course of wars or rituals. Although sachems in theory possessed ultimate authority over the group, they had no way of enforcing this authority except through the use of persuasion and diplomacy.

smallpox

Smallpox is a virus that causes fever, muscle ache, vomiting, and a telltale rash that consists of oozing pustules. Because Native Americans had never been exposed to the disease before and had no measure of immunity, they died in enormous numbers when the disease was introduced by European colonists. Although transmission of the disease to Native Americans was usually accidental, there is evidence to suggest that on at least one occasion blankets infected with smallpox were intentionally given to Native Americans to start an epidemic.

wampum

Wampum were shell beads crafted by Native Americans and used as a form of money, ornamentation, and diplomatic exchange. Wampum was made from the shells of welk clams and could be white or purple. The exchange of wampum was often used to cement the bond between allied Native American groups. The introduction of metal European tools made it much easier to produce wampum, and Native American groups on the coast set up simple factories to produce the highly sought after wampum. A six-foot string of purple wampum beads was worth approximately 12 shillings.

Biographies

Benjamin Church

Born in 1639 in Plymouth colony, New England soldier and frontiersman Benjamin Church was a proponent of adopting the so-called skulking way of war practiced by Native Americans. He also favored using Native American allies to defeat King Philip and his supporters during King Philip's War. On August 12, 1676, Church and his band of colonials and natives tracked down and killed King Philip, essentially bringing an end to the conflict. Church later served in King William's War and Queen Anne's War, during which he and his men often attacked the villages of Native Americans allied with the French. Church often clashed with colonial leaders over the treatment of Native American prisoners, who Church believed should not be sold into slavery. His memoirs garnered significant attention because of the emphasis Church placed on the role of personal agency—rather than divine will—in determining English victories in the many colonial struggles. Church died on January 17, 1717, in Rhode Island.

John Mason

John Mason was born around 1600 in England. He served in the English army before journeying to North America in 1632. When war broke out between the colonists and the Pequot Confederacy, Mason was selected to lead a force of volunteers against the powerful Pequots. Commanding some 90 colonials and 60 Mohegans led by Uncas, Mason attacked the main Pequot settlement, known as Mystic Fort, on May 26, 1637. The attackers set fire to the fort, and some 800 Pequot men, women, and children perished in the attack. Afterward, Mason and his men hunted down and captured a number of the survivors from the Mystic Fort Fight. From the Pequot War until the end of his life, one of Mason's chief duties was negotiating with local Native American groups. Mason died in Norwich, Connecticut, sometime in 1672.

Massasoit

Massasoit was born about 1590 near present-day Bristol, Rhode Island. He served as the grand sachem of the Wampanoags during much of the 17th century. Massasoit is remembered for his alliance with the Pilgrims and his efforts to aid the Plymouth colony. Concern over the possibility of conflict with the neighboring Narragansetts led Massasoit to forge an alliance with the colonists at Plymouth in March 1621. The resulting treaty was mutually beneficial, providing security for the colonists and military aid for the Wampanoags in case of hostilities with the Narragansetts. This allowed the Wampanoags to remain out of the Pequot War and staved off attempts at Christianization. To ensure continued peace between the Wampanoags and Massachusetts, Massasoit agreed to sell land to the colonists. Massasoit died in 1661 or 1662. His son, Metacomet, known as King Philip, launched King Philip's War in 1675.

Groups and Organizations

Algonquins

During the 17th century, the Algonquins, a Native American people, occupied the area on the border between the present-day Canadian provinces of Ontario and Quebec. The Algonquins were part of a larger Algonquian linguistic group that included many other Native American tribes. At the time of first European contact in 1603, the Algonquins numbered approximately 6,000 people, but by 1768 this number had fallen to only 1,500. The Algonquins became allied with the French in the early 17th century and for a time dominated the fur trade in the Saint Lawrence River Valley. Because of both their dealings with the French and long-standing disputes, the Algonquins found themselves in constant conflict with the Iroquois Confederacy, especially the Mohawks. Although initially fighting with the French during the French and Indian War, the Algonquins agreed to adopt a neutral stance after British and colonial forces took control of Quebec in 1760. Subsequently, the Algonquins fought on the side of the British during the American Revolutionary War and the War of 1812.

Massachusetts Bay colony

The Massachusetts Bay colony was founded in New England by the Massachusetts Bay Company. Although initially intended as a business venture, the colony's intended purpose changed in 1629 when England began persecuting Puritans. The first group of about 1,000 settlers, led by John Winthrop, arrived in North America in 1630 and established Boston, around which the colony would grow. About one-fifth of the settlers died during the first year, but Massachusetts Bay would eventually become an extremely prosperous colony. Although thoroughly theocratic, the colony developed into a representative democracy that was entirely self-governing. It functioned under very strict religious rules and did not hesitate to expel individuals deemed morally questionable, including Anne Hutchinson and Roger Williams. As the colony prospered, however, its members gradually became less devoutly Puritan. In 1684, the Massachusetts Bay Company lost its charter, and in 1691 Boston and the surrounding area became a royal colony.

Mohegans

An Algonquian-speaking Native American group, the Mohegans lived in New England during the 17th century and are often confused today with the distinctively separate Mahicans. Originally a subgroup of the Pequots, the Mohegans were a seminomadic people who hunted, fished, and grew crops. Uncas, a noted Mohegan sachem, established friendly relations with the English colonists. After the colonial victory in the Pequot War, the Mohegans, who claimed much of the Pequots' land, became a powerful group. During King Philip's War, the Mohegans fought on the side of the colonists, and Mohegan warriors were present at the devastating Great

Continues on next page

Swamp Fight, which killed hundreds of Narragansetts. The Mohegans remained constant allies of the English during the many colonial wars with France. Even so, English colonists took much of the Mohegans' land and even sold some of them into slavery. European diseases also reduced the Mohegans' numbers. The group eventually resettled on a reservation in Wisconsin in the 1820s.

Narragansetts

During the 17th century, the Narragansetts were a powerful Native American group that had authority over many other native peoples in southeastern New England. Initially, the Narragansett enjoyed friendly relations with the English colonists of New England and even fought for them during the Pequot War. Relations soured after this point, however, and during the 1640s the Narragansetts were forced to submit to English and colonial authority in order to avoid war. Although the Narragansetts attempted to remain neutral during the beginning stages of King Philip's War, the colonists began attacking Narragansett settlements. This offensive culminated in the devastating Great Swamp Fight of December 19, 1675, in which more than 600 Narragansetts died. After that, the Narragansetts openly aided King Philip and his allies. After the war, the Narragansetts ceased to exist as an independent entity, joining with the Niantics and working to assimilate into American culture as the only means to survive.

New England Confederation

The New England Confederation was a union of four New England colonies, first chartered on September 7, 1643, that lasted, despite several periods of stagnation, until 1691. Also known as the United Colonies of New England, it included the colonies of Connecticut, Massachusetts Bay, Plymouth, and New Haven and marked the first attempt at a European-style federation in North America. Colonial officials founded the confederation chiefly to provide protection from the threat presented by Native Americans and other European colonizing powers. It was also intended to mediate boundary disputes between the confederated colonies. Although it had no power to compel its members to act, the confederation proved an important institution during several conflicts with Native Americans, including King Philip's War. Although not officially dissolved until 1691, when Massachusetts became a royal colony, the confederation occasionally ceased to function as a legitimate political entity because of conflicts between its member colonies.

Pequot Confederacy

A powerful Native American group that lived along the Connecticut River during the 17th century, the Pequots dominated other tribes, forcing them to pay tribute to a grand sachem. By the 1630s, the confederation consisted of some 26 groups. The Pequots fought the first major Native American war against New England settlers over control of land. In 1636, after several relatively minor Native American attacks, the colonists embarked on a devastating offensive, burning Pequot villages and fields. The climactic engagement of the Pequot War came on May 26, 1637, when colonial and allied native forces attacked and burned the fortified settlement known as Mystic Fort. Some 800 Pequots, including many women and children, were killed. After the massacre, the survivors who were not hunted down and killed or sold into slavery escaped to neighboring Native American groups. The remaining Pequots formally gave up their land and rights in the Treaty of Hartford, signed in September 1638.

Wampanoags

A Native American group, the Wampanoags inhabited an area ranging from the eastern shore of Narragansett Bay to the tip of Cape Cod during the 17th century. The Wampanoags were farmers, fishermen, hunters, and gatherers. At the time of first European contact, they numbered approximately 12,000, although European diseases had decreased their numbers to only 2,000 by 1620. The Wampanoags also fell prey to conflicts with other native groups, such as the Micmacs and the Pequots. To help bolster the group's position, Massasoit, a noted Wampanoag leader, entered into a treaty with the colonists of Plymouth in 1621 that benefited both parties. The death of Massasoit, however, ushered in dramatic change in the leadership of the Wampanoags. His son, Metacomet, known as King Philip, was the Wampanoag leader when the tribe became embroiled in King Philip's War (1675–1676). The Wampanoags suffered horribly during the war, and by the end of the short conflict there were only several hundred survivors, many of whom had been sold into slavery.

Events

American Indian Wars

The American Indian Wars took place in the period between roughly 1500 and 1890 and can be divided into four periods. The first set of wars took place primarily between Native Americans and Spanish conquistadors and missionaries during the 16th and 17th centuries in what would become the southwestern United States. The second series of wars occurred in the 17th century along the eastern seaboard and across what would become the border between Canada and the United States. This set of wars, which included King Philip's War and the French and Indian War, were fought between Native Americans and various European colonists representing the interests of England, France, and the Netherlands. The third set of wars occurred in the early 19th century, as Anglo-American settlements intruded deeper into Florida and the interior of the Ohio and Mississippi valleys, and would include the Creek Wars and the Seminole Wars. The final battles of the American Indian Wars occurred in the late 19th century, primarily on the Great Plains and in the southwestern United States, and would include the Red River War and the Battle of Little Bighorn.

Bloody Brook Massacre

In mid-September 1675, as King Philip's War worsened, colonial officials decided to abandon certain outlying towns, including Deerfield, Massachusetts. Captain Thomas Lathrop was ordered to protect a caravan of wagons moving Deerfield's large supplies of drying corn to safety in Springfield. Lathrop was confident they would not be bothered by any Native Americans. Yet when the caravan had reached Muddy Brook, about five miles south of Deerfield, on September 19, Lathrop, the militiamen, and the cart drivers found themselves suddenly surrounded by hundreds of Wampanoags, Nipmucks, and other Native Americans. In just a few minutes, the attackers killed at least 60 colonials, including Lathrop. As the survivors staggered back to Deerfield, they were taunted by Native Americans but were not attacked. The incident shocked the colonists, and afterward the stream became known as Bloody Brook.

Burning of Springfield

On October 5, 1675, warriors of the Agawam tribe—believed by the colonists to be friendly or at the least neutral—attacked Springfield, Massachusetts. The town was virtually undefended, as the community's militiamen had left to join a large expedition against hostile Native Americans. The residents did, however, have some advance warning of the attack and so were able to withdraw safely to fortified garrison houses. They could do nothing, however, to prevent warriors from burning the settlement's undefended houses, barns, and outbuildings. On learning of the attack, two colonial forces immediately marched south to relieve Springfield. The attacking Agawams, who had been reinforced by Nipmuck warriors, then withdrew. The colonists suffered only three dead and three or four wounded in the attack. Nevertheless, the town was virtually destroyed.

Great Swamp Fight

Although the Narragansetts were officially neutral during King Philip's War, colonial leaders believed some Narragansett warriors were secretly joining Wampanoag leader King Philip's raiding parties and that the tribe itself was harboring wounded warriors. Determined to put an end to such assistance, the commissioners of the New England Confederation assembled the largest colonial force America had seen to that point. On December 19, 1675, the force reached the Narragansetts' Great Swamp Fortress. When they could not take the fort through sheer force, the colonials decided to burn it. Although some warriors escaped into the woods, many more natives—mostly women, children, and the elderly—died in the fire. Estimates of Native American dead ranged from 600 to as many as 1,000. Twenty colonials were killed and some 200 were wounded. The attack prompted the remaining members of the Narragansett tribe to join King Philip in his fight against the English colonists.

King Philip's War

The last and deadliest general war between Native Americans and English colonists in southern New England, this conflict was named for Wampanoag sachem Metacomet, known to the colonists as King Philip. Although tensions between the Native Americans and the English colonists had been building for years, the murder of the informant John Sassamon in January 1675, and the subsequent arrest and execution of three Wampanoag warriors for the crime in early June, provided the spark that ignited full-scale hostilities. Fighting quickly spread throughout New England. A number of tribes would eventually join the Wampanoags, specifically the Narragansett, Pocasset, Sakonnet, and Nipmuck peoples. Important engagements of the war included the native attack on Swansea, the burning of Springfield, the ambush at Bloody Brook and the colonial massacre of Native American men, women, and children in the Great Swamp Fight. When King Philip was killed on August 12, 1676, Native American resistance soon died with him.

Continues on next page

Mystic Fort Fight

The Mystic Fort Fight involved an assault on a palisaded Pequot community near the Mystic River in present-day Connecticut on May 26, 1637. The attack was carried out by a force of English settlers and their Mohegan and Narragansett allies. When Pequot warriors attacked the settlement of Wethersfield in late April 1637, killing nine people and capturing two girls, the colony of Connecticut declared war. A force of some 90 men under Captain John Mason marched on the large Pequot settlement on the Mystic River. Joined by several hundred Native American warriors, Mason's group attacked the Pequots. Finding the fighting difficult, they decided to set the settlement on fire. Between 400 and 700 Pequots died in the battle and conflagration. English casualties for the campaign amounted to two killed and 20 wounded; casualties among their native allies are unknown. After the attack, many more Pequots were hunted down and either killed or sold into slavery.

Pequot War

The Pequot War grew out of growing tensions between the Pequots and English settlers in Connecticut and Massachusetts Bay as both sides expanded their power and influence. The deaths of a colonial trader and captain, however, spurred the colonists to action. In August 1636, Massachusetts dispatched a force of some 90 captains, led by captains John Endicott and John Underhill, to attack Native American settlements. The expedition burned villages and crops, and the Native Americans retaliated by attacking colonial settlements such as Fort Saybrook. Attacks and counterattacks continued until May 26, 1637, when a colonial force led by John Mason attacked and burned the fortified Pequot settlement on the Mystic River, killing hundreds of men, women, and children. Although sporadic fighting continued, Pequot resistance was largely broken. The Treaty of Hartford, signed on September 21, 1638, officially ended the Pequot War. With it, the Pequots ceased to exist as an independent people.

Siege of Brookfield

On August 2, 1675, a party of colonists with Native American guides left the central Massachusetts town of Brookfield to meet with local sachems. When the sachems failed to arrive at the appointed time and place, the group went in search of them, and in so doing fell into an ambush prepared by Nipmuck warriors. The survivors of this attack retreated to Brookfield and, with residents of the town, defended themselves during the ensuing siege in the settlement's garrison house. During the siege, the Nipmucks repeatedly tried to set the garrison house on fire, although their plans were foiled by rain. The Nipmucks abandoned their assault on August 5 when colonial militiamen arrived. The siege made it clear to the colonists that other Native American groups in addition to the Wampanoags would join in King Philip's War against New England.

Tecumseh and the Westward Movement

Tecumseh and the Westward Movement

▲ Tecumseh was a well-known Shawnee military leader in the early 19th century. Image created/published between 1860 and 1900. (Library of Congress)

In the second half of the 18th century, Anglo-American settlers moved deeper into the interior of the Ohio and Mississippi river valleys, sparking hostilities with the Native American tribes in those regions. One of the tribes, the Shawnees, was very active in fighting against the British. Many Shawnee warriors participated in Pontiac's Rebellion, which erupted in 1763 after the end of the French and Indian War.

The Shawnee chief Cornstalk led raids against frontier settlements in Virginia during the rebellion, but when it ended he decided the best course of action was to try to maintain peaceful relations with the English. Cornstalk's efforts at diplomacy came to an end in 1774, when Virginia governor Lord Dunmore dispatched soldiers to the Ohio River Valley after a series of frontier murders and revenge raids. Although Cornstalk counseled peace, the Shawnees voted to attack the invaders. After the Shawnees suffered a humiliating defeat, Cornstalk agreed to British peace terms, bringing an end to Lord Dunmore's War. Despite that loss, the Shawnees joined the British cause in the American Revolution after being pressured by the colonies to cede land.

One of the casualties of Lord Dunmore's War was Shawnee war chief Pukeshinwa, the father of Tecumseh and the Prophet. After Pukeshinwa was killed, Tecumseh made clear his hatred for whites and joined raiding parties as soon as he was old enough to fight. When the American Revolutionary War ended in 1783, the pace of westward migration increased, creating more conflict between white settlers and American Indians. Tecumseh was active in the fighting, and by the end of the decade he had established himself as a top scout and warrior under prominent Shawnee war chief Blue Jacket. After Blue Jacket was defeated at the Battle of Fallen Timbers in 1794, Tecumseh would not admit defeat and refused to sign the Treaty of Greenville the following year. With a small group of followers, including his brother, the Prophet, Tecumseh left Ohio for the relative safety of the Indiana Territory.

In the early 19th century, Tecumseh and Tenskwatawa earned reputations as two of the last great military defenders of Indian land in the entire region. Known as "The Shawnee Prophet," Tenskwatawa's popularity stemmed from his activities as a shaman, and he advocated for American Indians to return to their traditions and give up such nonnative elements as alcohol and Christianity. Tecumseh, who had become a top military strategist and a talented orator, began to use his brother's religious teachings as the basis for a pan-Indian movement to establish an Indian nation along the western border of the United States to prevent its further expansion. In 1808, Tecumseh and Tenskwatawa moved their followers to a new village at the junction of the Tippecanoe and Wabash rivers in western Indiana and named the settlement Prophetstown.

In September 1809, Indiana territorial governor William Henry Harrison forced the Native Americans in Indiana to sign the Treaty of Fort Wayne, ceding huge tracts of land in the region to the white Americans. Tecumseh strongly opposed the treaty, arguing that the land belonged to all Native Americans and could not be sold without the consent of all. Tecumseh began traveling widely to recruit followers, going as far south as Florida and as far west as Iowa. Meanwhile, Harrison decided to strike a serious blow against the two brothers by destroying Prophetstown. In the fall of 1811, he led an army outside the village but delayed his attack when a Native American delegation requested negotiations. Ignoring the absent Tecumseh's orders to avoid a fight until the Indian confederation was secure, Tenskwatawa launched a surprise attack early in the morning on November 7. Harrison's troops suffered heavy losses but were able to repel the Indian attack and destroy Prophetstown.

The Battle of Tippecanoe damaged Tenskwatawa's reputation and was a major setback to his brother's vision of building a confederation to stave off white settlement. When Tecumseh returned, he and his brother had

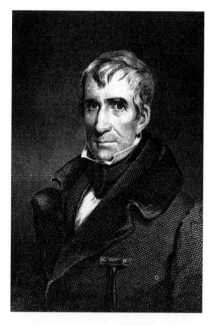

▲ William Henry Harrison, governor of the Indiana Territory and later president of the United States. Painting by James R. Lambdin. (Library of Congress)

▶ The Prophet and Tecumseh at Prophetstown, which was founded by the brothers in 1808 as the center for Tecumseh's pan-Indian movement. The town was burned during the Battle of Tippecanoe in November 1811, and the rebuilt settlement was later destroyed by the Kentucky militia in November 1812. (Library of Congress)

a falling out, and Tecumseh was never able to recover the momentum behind his pan-Indian movement after the battle, despite support from the Red Sticks of Alabama. Tecumseh joined the British cause in the War of 1812, hoping that what remained of his alliance, in conjunction with British forces, could defeat the United States. Although Tecumseh led many successful campaigns, many Indians refused to join the war. When Tecumseh was killed during the Battle of the Thames in October 1813, his dream of a unified Native American state perished with him. Tenskwatawa lived in Canada after the War of 1812. When he returned to the United States in 1835, he helped the U.S. government move many Shawnees west of the Mississippi River.

Tecumseh and the Westward Movement

AUTHOR

CHRIS MULLIN
Santa Ynez Valley
Union High School

AUTHOR

BRETT PIERSMA
Santa Ynez Valley
Union High School

This section of the resource book will focus on the years 1805–1815 and will take place in five stages. The primary focus will be the interaction between the Shawnee Indian leaders, Tecumseh and his brother, the Prophet, and Indiana territorial governor William Henry Harrison and the U.S. federal government. The unit will investigate strategic and political elements surrounding the Battle of Tippecanoe and the Battle of the Thames as well as relationships within the various Indian tribes of the Old Northwest. Likewise, the activities will shed light on the role played by Great Britain in these military hostilities.

Lesson 1 Students will become immersed in the words of the historical figures as they unravel the military and political events that took place in the early 19th century. The students will gain insight into the cultural impressions, biases, and viewpoints felt by both the Anglo and Indian protagonists.

Lesson 2 Students will play the role of military historians, piecing together a real battlefield using only the words of those who observed the event. Students will complete the activity by drafting their own map with a bird's-eye view of the event and then comparing it to a modern map of the same battle.

Lesson 3 Students will investigate England's role in the war by dissecting both written and visual evidence related to English participation. As part of the lesson, students will redesign an anti-British political cartoon.

Lesson 4 Students will take part in a detailed analysis of an Anglo American painting of the Battle of the Thames. They will dissect the style of imagery and captioning to understand the cultural biases in the illustration.

Lesson 5 This final lesson is designed to humanize Tecumseh while revealing his frustration with his British allies. Students will gain a final glimpse into Tecumseh's personality by reading two very different writings. The first was written just before his final battle, and in it he criticizes the British for abandoning his cause. The second is a poem of reflection on dying. Students will pull together all that they have experienced in the previous activities.

LESSON 1
Voices from the Past

MATERIALS NEEDED

HANDOUT

- Ten Quotations from Different Perspectives, pp. 105–108

HISTORIAN ANALYSIS WORKSHEETS

- **Portraits** of Tecumseh, the Prophet, and William Henry Harrison, p. 109
- The **Words** of Tecumseh, the Prophet, and William Henry Harrison, p. 110
- **Accounts** of Tecumseh, the Prophet, and William Henry Harrison, p. 111

IMAGES

- Tecumseh, p. 129
- The Prophet, p. 130

- Indiana Territorial Governor William Henry Harrison, p. 131

DOCUMENTS

- Passage Written by Tecumseh to William Henry Harrison, 1810, p. 132
- Passage Written by the Prophet to William Henry Harrison, 1808, p. 133
- Passages Written by William Henry Harrison, p. 134
- Passage about Tecumseh by William Henry Harrison, p. 135
- Passage about the Prophet by Thomas Jefferson, p. 136
- Passage about William Henry Harrison by Isaac Rand Jackson, p. 137

DEBATE INSTRUCTIONS

- Team Indiana Territorial Governor, William Henry Harrison, pp. 112–113
- Team U.S. Secretary of War William Eustis (Representing President James Madison), pp. 114–115
- Team the Prophet, Shawnee Brother of Tecumseh, pp. 116–117
- Team Choctaw Chief Pushmataha (Response to Tecumseh), pp. 118–119
- Team Tecumseh, pp. 120–121

HISTORICAL BACKGROUND

- The Shawnee Brothers: Tecumseh and the Prophet, pp. 138–139

This lesson takes place in three parts, all designed to help students unravel the military and political events that took place in the early part of the 19th century and gain insight into the cultural impressions, biases, and viewpoints felt by both the Anglo and Indian protagonists.

Step One

The purpose of this step is to introduce students to an era of conflict between Native and European Americans. Students are asked to read aloud historical quotes by individuals living at the time of Tecumseh and the Prophet, and then work in teams to place those quotes in categories. This process allows students to reflect on value judgments held by both groups and predict the opinions each group held about the other. It is a quick, anticipatory introduction into the larger themes in the lesson.

Continues on next page

Lesson 1

Voices from the Past, Continued

First the teacher should post the Ten Quotations from Different Perspectives handout in different places around the room. All 10 quotations came from the era of the U.S. war with Tecumseh and the Prophet. Students should walk around the room in groups of two or three and read each quote to themselves. Each small group should start at a different quotation and then advance every minute or so, moving clockwise to the next quotation. The teacher should instruct students to try to divide the documents into two categories with an equal number of documents in each: Words of European Americans and Words of Native Americans. The correct answers are Words of European Americans, quotes 2, 3, 5, 8, 10, and Words of Native Americans, quotes 1, 4, 6, 7, 9.

Step Two

This step allows students to read and reflect on the values of Tecumseh, the Prophet, and William Henry Harrison, three individuals who play a dominant role in the following lessons. The teacher should divide the class into thirds; each group will be responsible for learning about one person, either Tecumseh, the Prophet, or Indiana governor William Henry Harrison. Then the teacher should distribute the appropriate image of each historical figure to the students in each group, along with the Historian Observation Worksheet, Analyzing Portraits of Tecumseh, the Prophet, and Governor William Henry Harrison. All three images are by different white male artists. The worksheet will help students focus on the personality traits they see in the individuals as well as artist bias. When the class has had time to complete their individual worksheets, the teacher should ask each third of the class to report back to the whole group about their findings.

Next, each third of the class will read a passage written by the same figure they observed in the previous picture activity. The teacher should distribute the documents Passage Written by Tecumseh to Governor William Henry Harrison to the Tecumseh group, Passage Written by the Prophet to Governor William Henry Harrison to the Prophet group, and Passages Written by Harrison to the Harrison group. Each group should also be given the Historian Analysis Worksheet, The Words of Tecumseh, the Prophet, and William Henry Harrison, and they will complete it for the person assigned to their group.

Finally, students will read and analyze documents written by others about these three individuals, so that upon completion of this step, students will have a deep understanding of who these historical figures were and the context of the times. The teacher should distribute the documents, Passage about Tecumseh by William Henry Harrison, Passage about the Prophet by Thomas Jefferson, and Passage about William Henry Harrison by Isaac Rand Jackson. Students should also be given the Historian Analysis Worksheet, Accounts of Tecumseh, the Prophet, and William Henry Harrison, and they will complete it for the person assigned to their group.

Lesson 1

Voices from the Past, Continued

Step Three

In this final activity students will discover various viewpoints on whether or not it would be desirable for Indians to join with Tecumseh and his Indian confederation versus the U.S. government. In this lesson all students but 10 will play the role of Indians who are undecided about which side to join in the developing conflict between the U.S. government and the Shawnee Indian brothers Tecumseh and the Prophet. Ten students will use primary sources to write and deliver speeches to convince the undecided Indians to join their side. The undecided students will read an overview of the issue and vote on what to do. Whichever side (U.S. government or Tecumseh/the Prophet) gains more of the undecided Indian votes wins.

This activity mimics the actual discussions that were going on at the time. Tecumseh worked tirelessly to recruit tribes and warriors to his cause. His ultimate goal was to reclaim lands in the Old Northwest that the Native Americans had lost to white settlement. Many local Indian tribes of the time were divided over which side to join. Many were also interested in joining the English Canadians, as some ended up doing when the War of 1812 broke out after the Battle of Tippecanoe. (The English voice is not, however, represented in this debate.)

The teacher should begin this activity by creating five teams of two students each. Those selected should be students who are the most likely to be comfortable with speaking aloud in class and writing an on-task speech. Each of the five pairs will represent the viewpoint of a different historical person after reading real speeches or letters written by those historical people. When the student teams are speaking, they should present themselves as the historical figure whose words they are reading. They should speak in the present tense and in the first person. They may read from a prepared speech or use a note card. The five different teams will represent Indiana governor William Henry Harrison, U.S. secretary of war William Eustis representing President James Madison, the Prophet, Choctaw chief Pushmataha, and Tecumseh.

Once the five teams have been created, the teacher should provide each one with two copies of their appropriate Debate Instructions. The handout includes specific directions for the pairs as well as an excerpt from a primary source written by their historical figure.

Continues on next page

DEFINING MOMENT II

Lesson 1

Voices from the Past, Continued

While the 10 students are preparing their speeches, the remaining students should read the Historical Background overview, The Shawnee Brothers: Tecumseh, and the Prophet, which will be helpful to their understanding of the debate.

When the five teams finish writing their persuasive speeches, the teacher should prepare the room and students for the debate. On one side of the room, the teacher should place the 10 students, seated in pairs, at a table or desks with name placards in front of them (Harrison, Eustis, Tecumseh, etc.) On the other side of the room, facing the 10 seated historical figures, the teacher should place the remaining students. These students represent undecided Indians.

The teacher should tell the students representing the Indians that they are about to hear from five historical figures, all of whom will try to convince them to join or not to join Tecumseh and the Prophet. Tell them that once they have heard all the speeches, they will be asked to vote. The vote may be taken by secret ballot or by dividing to one side or another of the classroom.

Lesson 1, Handout
Ten Quotations from Different Perspectives

Quotation 1

"When it comes your time to die, be not like those whose hearts are filled with fear of death . . .
Sing your death song and die like a hero going home."

Source: Bent, Devin. "Tecumseh: A Brief Biography." Available from The James Madison Center, *http://www.jmu.edu/madison/center/main_pages/madison_archives/era/native/tecumseh/bio.htm*

Quotation 2

"Where's your captain?"	*"Dead, sir."*
"Your first lieutenant?"	*"Dead, sir."*
"Your second lieutenant?"	*"Dead, sir."*
"Your ensign?"	*"Here, sir!"*

Source: Tunnell, Harry D. *To Compel with Armed Force: A Staff Ride Handbook for the Battle of Tippecanoe.* Available from the Combined Arms Research Library, *http://wwwcgsc.army.mil/carl/resources/csi/tunnell/tunnell.asp*

Continues on next page

Lesson 1, Handout

Ten Quotations from Different Perspectives, Continued

Quotation 3

"Sam, sleep with your moccasins on, for them red devils are going to fight before day."

Source: Tunnell, Harry D. *To Compel with Armed Force: A Staff Ride Handbook for the Battle of Tippecanoe.* Available from the Combined Arms Research Library, *http://wwwcgsc.army.mil/carl/resources/csi/tunnell/ tunnell.asp*

Quotation 4

"I am a Shawnee. My forefathers were warriors. Their son is a warrior. From them I only take my existence. From my tribe I take nothing. I am the maker of my own fortune."

Source: Bryan, William Jennings. *The World's Famous Orations.* New York: Funk and Wagnalls, 1906. Available from *http://www.bartleby.com/268/8/4.html*

Quotation 5

"The troops, nineteen twentieths of whom had never been in action before behaved in a manner that can never be too much applauded."

Source: Tunnell, Harry D. *To Compel with Armed Force: A Staff Ride Handbook for the Battle of Tippecanoe.* Available from the Combined Arms Research Library, *http://www-cgsc.army.mil/carl/resources/csi/tunnell/ tunnell.asp*

Lesson 1, Handout

Ten Quotations from Different Perspectives, Continued

Quotation 6

"I saw some of the men shoot squirrels, as they rode along, and I said, the Indians have no such guns. These men will kill us as far as they can see."

Source: Tunnell, Harry D. *To Compel with Armed Force: A Staff Ride Handbook for the Battle of Tippecanoe.* Available from the Combined Arms Research Library, *http://www-cgsc.army.mil/carl/resources/csi/tunnell/tunnell.asp*

Quotation 7

"As soon as daylight came our warriors saw that the Prophet's grand plan had failed—that the great white chief was alive riding fearlessly among his troops in spite of bullets, and their hearts melted."

Source: Tunnell, Harry D. *To Compel with Armed Force: A Staff Ride Handbook for the Battle of Tippecanoe.* Available from the Combined Arms Research Library, *http://www-cgsc.army.mil/carl/resources/csi/tunnell/tunnell.asp*

Quotation 8

"The implicit obedience and respect which the followers of Tecumseh pay to him, is really astonishing, and more than any other circumstance bespeaks him one of those uncommon geniuses."

Source: Drake, Benjamin. *Life of Tecumseh, and His Brother the Prophet With a Historical Sketch of the Shawanoe Indians.* Available from Project Gutenberg, *http://www.gutenberg.org/ebooks/15581*

Continues on next page

Lesson 1, Handout

Ten Quotations from Different Perspectives, Continued

Quotation 9

"It is true he [President Jefferson] is so far off he will not be injured by the war. He may sit in his town and drink his wine, while you and I will have to fight it out."

Source: Drake, Benjamin. *Life of Tecumseh, and His Brother the Prophet With a Historical Sketch of the Shawanoe Indians.* Available from Project Gutenberg, *http://www.gutenberg.org/ebooks/15581*

Quotation 10

"The mind of a savage is so constructed that he cannot be at rest, he cannot be happy unless it is acted upon by some strong stimulus."

Source: Buff, Rachel. "Tecumseh and Tenskwatawa: Myth, Historiography and Popular Memory." *Historical Reflections* 21. (1995): 277–299.

Lesson 1, Historian Analysis Worksheet

Portraits of Tecumseh, the Prophet, and William Henry Harrison

Instructions: A picture can often reveal a great deal about an individual in history. Take a look at your assigned portrait and see if you can tell what kind of personalities these historical figures had. Also think about what message the artist was trying to get across. Get ready to share and compare!

1. How is your subject dressed? What does the clothing tell you about him?

_____

_____

2. What kind of expression does your subject have on his face?

_____

_____

3. What does the subject's posture or body language tell you about his personality?

_____

_____

4. What are three adjectives that describe the subject?

_____

_____

5. Summarize the personality of your subject in a sentence or two.

_____

_____

6. Do you think the artist has included his personal bias or cultural opinions? Explain.

_____

_____

Lesson 1, Historian Analysis Worksheet

The **Words** of Tecumseh, the Prophet, and William Henry Harrison

Instructions: Now that you have analyzed a portrait of your historical person, try to figure out what he is like from his own words.

1. Do your subject's own words seem to paint a similar picture to the one you just observed?

_____

_____

_____

_____

_____

2. What character traits do your subject's own words present?

_____

_____

_____

_____

_____

3. What issues are important to your subject?

_____

_____

_____

_____

_____

Lesson 1, Historian Analysis Worksheet

Accounts of Tecumseh, the Prophet, and William Henry Harrison

Instructions: Now that you have analyzed a portrait of your historical figure and read his own words, read a short description by someone who lived during the same time period.

1. Does the description agree with your opinions about your subject?

_____

_____

_____

_____

_____

2. How is this written observation similar? Different?

_____

_____

_____

_____

_____

3. Do you like this historical figure? Why? Why not?

_____

_____

_____

_____

_____

Lesson 1, Debate Instructions

Team Indiana Territorial Governor William Henry Harrison

Task: You are about to address a group of Indians from your own territory of Indiana. Many of these Indians are considering joining with the Shawnee brothers Tecumseh and the Prophet in their attempt to unify all Indians and reclaim lands the Indians have lost to white settlers. You are determined to convince them that joining with Tecumseh and the Prophet will only spell their doom. Make reference to the strength of your military and the numbers of your people. Likewise, you wish to show that you are a reasonable and caring leader who wants what's best for them. You are especially disturbed that they have taken an interest in the Prophet's brand of religion.

Use both ideas and actual quotations from the passages presented here to make a persuasive speech that you will read aloud to the assembled Indians. The speech must be no fewer than 200 words, 100 of which must be in your own words and 100 of which should be in the form of direct quotes from the two passages. Write in the first person and in the present tense, making use of "I" statements. You may both take turns reading or select one reader. You may write more than 200 words if you wish.

Passage 1

My children: My heart is filled with grief and my eyes are dissolved in tears at the news which has reached me. You have been celebrated for your wisdom above all the tribes of the red people who inhabit this great island. Your fame as warriors has extended to the remotest nations, and the wisdom of your chiefs has gained you the appellation of grandfathers from all the neighboring tribes. From what cause, then, does it proceed that you have departed from the wise council of your fathers, and covered yourselves with guilt? My children, tread back the steps you have taken, and endeavor to regain the straight road you have abandoned. The dark, crooked and thorny one which you are now pursuing will certainly lead to endless woe and misery. But who is this pretended prophet who dares to speak in the name of the great Creator? Examine him. Is he more wise and virtuous than you are yourselves, that he should be selected to convey to you the orders of your God? Demand of him some proof at least of his being the messenger of the Deity. If God has really employed him, He has doubtless authorized him to perform miracles that he may be known and received as a prophet. If he is really a prophet, ask him to cause the sun to stand still, or the moon to alter its courses, the river to cease to flow or the dead to rise from their graves. If he does these things you may believe that he is sent from God. He tells you that the Great Spirit commands you to punish with death those who deal in magic, and that he is authorized to point them out. Wretched delusion! Is, then, the Master of Life compelled to employ mortal man to punish those who offend Him? Has He not the thunder and the power of nature at his command? And could not He sweep away from the earth

Lesson 1, Debate Instructions

Team Indiana Territorial Governor William Henry Harrison, Continued

the whole nation at one motion of His arm? My children, do not believe that the great and good Creator has directed you to destroy your own flesh, and do not doubt that if you pursue this abominable wickedness, His vengeance will overtake you and crush you. The above is addressed to you in the name of the Seventeen Fires. I now speak to you from myself, as a friend who wishes you nothing more sincerely than to see you prosperous and happy. Clear your eyes, I beseech you, from the mist which surrounds them. No longer be imposed upon by the arts of an impostor. Drive him from your town and let peace and harmony prevail amongst you. Let your poor old men and women sleep in quietness, and banish from their minds the dreadful idea of being burnt alive by their own friends and countrymen. I charge you to stop your bloody career, and if you value the friendship of your great father, the president, if you wish to preserve the good opinion of the Seventeen Fires, let me hear by the return of the bearer that you are determined to follow my advice."

Source: Drake, Benjamin. *Life of Tecumseh, and His Brother the Prophet With a Historical Sketch of the Shawanoe Indians.* Available from Project Gutenberg, *http://www.gutenberg.org/ebooks/15581*

Passage 2

The chain of friendship which united the whites and the Indians, may be renewed and be as strong as ever. A great deal of that works depends on you—the destiny of those who are under your direction, depends upon the choice you make of the two roads which are before you. The one is large, open and pleasant and leads to peace, security and happiness; the other, on the contrary, is narrow and crooked and leads to misery and ruin. Don't deceive yourselves; do not believe that all nations of Indians united are able to resist the force of the Seventeen Fires. I know your warriors are brave, but ours are not less so. But what can a few brave warriors do against the innumerable warriors of the Seventeen Fires? Our blue-coats are more numerous than you can count. Our hunters are like the leaves of the forest or the grains of sand on the Wabash. Do not think that the red-coats can protect you; they are not able to protect themselves. They do not think of going to war with us. If they did, you would in a few moons see our flag wave over all the forts of Canada.

Note: The phrase "Seventeen Fires" refers to the 17 U.S. states that existed at this time.

Source: Drake, Benjamin. *Life of Tecumseh, and His Brother the Prophet With a Historical Sketch of the Shawanoe Indians.* Available from Project Gutenberg, *http://www.gutenberg.org/ebooks/15581*

Lesson 1, Debate Instructions
Team U.S. Secretary of War William Eustis (Representing President James Madison)

Task: You are about to address a group of Indians in the Indiana Territory. Many of these Indians are considering joining with the Shawnee brothers Tecumseh and the Prophet in their attempt to unify all Indians and to reclaim lands the Indians have lost to white settlers. You are determined to convince them that joining with Tecumseh and the Prophet will only spell their doom. Make reference to the strength of the military and President Madison's determination to use force. You are especially disturbed by the actions and organization of the Prophet. Make it clear that you fully intend to capture him if necessary and will punish any wrongdoing. You will also hold accountable any accomplices. Essentially, your job is not to make friends but rather to point out the very weak power position the Indians are in should they choose to join Tecumseh and the Prophet.

Use both ideas and actual quotations from the passages presented here to make a persuasive speech that you will read aloud to the assembled Indians. The speech must be no fewer than 200 words, 100 of which must be in your own words and 100 of which should be in the form of direct quotes from the three passages. Write in the first person and in the present tense, making use of "I" statements. You may both take turns reading or select one reader. You may write more than 200 words if you wish.

Passage 1

I have been particularly instructed by the President to communicate to your Excellency, his earnest desire that peace may, if possible, be preserved with the Indians, and that to this end every proper means may be adopted. By this it is not intended that murders or robberies committed by them, should not meet with punishment due to those crimes; that the settlements should be unprotected or that any hostile combination should avail itself of success in consequence of a neglect to provide the means of resisting and defeating it; or that the banditti under the Prophet should not be attacked and vanquished, providing such a measure should be rendered absolutely necessary. Circumstances conspire, at this particular juncture to render it peculiarly desirable that hostilities of any kind, or to any degree, not indispensably required, should be avoided.

Source: Drake, Benjamin. *Life of Tecumseh, and His Brother the Prophet With a Historical Sketch of the Shawanoe Indians.* Available from Project Gutenberg, *http://www.gutenberg.org/ebooks/15581*

Lesson 1, Debate Instructions

Team U.S. Secretary of War William Eustis (Representing President James Madison), Continued

Passage 2

The course to be pursued with the Prophet and his assemblage, must depend, in a great measure, if not wholly, on his conduct, and on the circumstances which occur as you approach him. You will approach and order him to disperse, which he may be permitted to do, on condition of satisfactory assurances that in future he shall not assemble or attempt to assemble any number of Indians, armed or hostile in attitude. If he neglects or refuses to disperse he will be attacked and compelled to it by the force under your command. He will probably in that case be taken prisoner. His adherents should be informed that in case they shall hereafter form any combination of a hostile nature, and oblige the government to send an armed force against them, they will be driven beyond the great waters, and never again permitted to live within the Jurisdictional limits of the United States. You will Judge the expediency of taking the chief or any of the associates as hostages. The objection to this measure appears to be, that it acknowledges the principal as an enemy entitled to respect, and implies the inconvenience of entering into & performing stipulations with a man of bad faith. A post may be established on the new purchase on the Wabash, if in your judgment it is required for the Security of the purchase or the Territories."

Source: Tunnell, Harry D. *To Compel with Armed Force: A Staff Ride Handbook for the Battle of Tippecanoe.* Available from the Combined Arms Research Library, *http://www-cgsc.army.mil/carl/resources/csi/tunnell/ tunnell.asp*

Passage 3

If the Prophet should commence, or seriously threaten hostilities, he ought to be attacked; provided the force under your command is sufficient to ensure success.

Source: Tunnell, Harry D. *To Compel with Armed Force: A Staff Ride Handbook for the Battle of Tippecanoe.* Available from the Combined Arms Research Library, *http://www-cgsc.army.mil/carl/resources/csi/tunnell/ tunnell.asp*

Lesson 1, Debate Instructions
Team the Prophet, Shawnee Brother of Tecumseh

Task: You are about to address a group of fellow Indians in the Indiana Territory. Many of these Indians are considering joining with you and your brother in your attempt to unify all Indians and to reclaim lands the Indians have lost to white settlers. You are determined to convince them that joining with Tecumseh and yourself is the only choice for the future survival of the Indian people. In your speech, however, you are going to celebrate all the good things about your religion, about its nonmilitary intentions, its avoidance of alcohol, and so on. Although these words were intended for the ears of President James Madison and Indiana governor William Henry Harrison, you will have to tailor them for the ears of fellow Indians. Try to come across as very reasonable and wishing only to share the blessings of "The Great Spirit" with your fellow Indians. Try to convince them that joining with you is a peaceful act.

Use both ideas and actual quotations from the passage presented here to make a persuasive speech that you will read aloud to the assembled Indians. The speech must be no fewer than 200 words, 100 of which must be in your own words and 100 of which should be in the form of direct quotes from the passage. Write in the first person and in the present tense, making use of "I" statements. You may both take turns reading or select one reader. You may write more than 200 words if you wish.

Passage

Father, It is three years since I first began with that system of religion which I now practice. The white people and some of the Indians were against me; but I had no other intention but to introduce among the Indians, those good principles of religion which the white people profess. I was spoken badly of by the white people, who reproached me with misleading the Indians; but I defy them to say that I did anything amiss. Father, I was told that you intended to hang me. When I heard this, I intended to remember it, and tell my father, when I went to see him, and relate to him the truth. I heard, when I settled on the Wabash, that my father, the governor, had declared that all the land between Vincennes and Fort Wayne, was the property of the Seventeen Fires. I also heard that you wanted to know, my father, whether I was God or man; and that you said if I was the former, I should not steal horses . . . The Great Spirit told me to tell the Indians that he had made them, and made the world—that he had placed them on it to do good, not evil. I told all the red skins, that the way they were in was not good, and that they ought to abandon it. That we ought to consider ourselves as one man; but we ought to live agreeably to our several customs, the red people after their mode, and the white people after theirs; partic-

Lesson 1, Debate Instructions

Team the Prophet, Shawnee Brother of Tecumseh, Continued

ularly, that they should not drink whiskey; that it was not made for them, but the white people, who alone knew how to use it; and that it is the cause of all the mischief which the Indians suffer; and that they must always follow the directions of the Great Spirit, and we must listen to him, as it was he that made us: determine to listen to nothing that is bad: do not take up the tomahawk, should it be offered by the British, or by the long knives: do not meddle with any thing that does not belong to you, but mind your own business, and cultivate the ground, that your women and your children may have enough to live on. I now inform you, that it is our intention to live in peace with our father and his people forever. My father, I have informed you what we mean to do, and I call the Great Spirit to witness the truth of my declaration. The religion which I have established for the last three years, has been attended to by the different tribes of Indians in this part of the world. Those Indians were once different people; they are now but one: they are all determined to practice what I have communicated to them, that has come immediately from the Great Spirit through me. Brother, I speak to you as a warrior. You are one. But let us lay aside this character, and attend to the care of our children, that they may live in comfort and peace. We desire that you will join us for the preservation of both red and white people. Formerly, when we lived in ignorance, we were foolish; but now, since we listen to the voice of the Great Spirit, we are happy. I have listened to what you have said to us. You have promised to assist us: I now request you, in behalf of all the red people, to use your exertions to prevent the sale of liquor to us. We are all well pleased to hear you say that you will endeavor to promote our happiness. We give you every assurance that we will follow the dictates of the Great Spirit. We are all well pleased with the attention that you have showed us; also with the good intentions of our father, the President."

Note: The phrase "Seventeen Fires" refers to the 17 U.S. states that existed at this time. The word "Father" here refers to both Governor William Henry Harrison and President James Madison.

Source: Drake, Benjamin. *Life of Tecumseh, and His Brother the Prophet With a Historical Sketch of the Shawanoe Indians.* Available from Project Gutenberg, *http://www.gutenberg.org/ebooks/15581*

Lesson 1, Debate Instructions
Team Choctaw Chief Pushmataha (Response to Tecumseh)

Task: You are about to address a group of fellow Indians in the Indiana Territory. Many of these Indians are considering joining with Tecumseh and the Prophet in their attempt to unify all Indians and to reclaim lands the Indians have lost to white settlers. You represent an older generation of Indians who still practice traditional clan or tribal values. You have seen too many Indians die in the many wars with the continually arriving white settlers. You are also uncomfortable about Tecumseh's desire to unify all Indians outside traditional tribal boundaries and the Prophet's new religion. Your basic view is that the overwhelming majority of Indians have no desire to join with the radical Shawnee brothers, Tecumseh, and the Prophet. You believe they are troublemakers stirring up the hatred of a minority of young warriors for a fruitless cause. Speak to these assembled Indians and convince them that the way of Tecumseh and the Prophet is wrong.

Use both ideas and actual quotations from the passage presented here to make a persuasive speech that you will read aloud to the assembled Indians. The speech must be no fewer than 200 words, 100 of which must be in your own words and 100 of which should be in the form of direct quotes from the passage. Write in the first person and in the present tense, making use of "I" statements. You may both take turns reading or select one reader. You may write more than 200 words if you wish.

Passage

Halt! Tecumseh, listen to me. You have come here, as you have often gone elsewhere, with a purpose to involve peaceful people in unnecessary trouble with their neighbors. Our people have no undue friction with the whites. Why? Because we have had no leaders stirring up strife to serve their selfish personal ambitions. You heard me say our people are a peaceful people. They make their way not by ravages upon their neighbor, but by honest toil. In that regard they have nothing in common with you. I know your history well. You are a disturber! You have ever been a trouble-maker. When you have found yourself unable to pick a quarrel with the white man, you have stirred up strife between different tribes of your own race. Not only that! You are a monarch, an unyielding tyrant within your own domain; every Shawnee, man, woman, and child must bow in submission to your imperious will. The Choctaws and Chickasaws have no monarchs. Their chieftains do not undertake the mastery of their people, but rather are they the people's servants, elected to serve the will of the majority. The majority has spoken on this question, and it has spoken against your contention. Their decision has, therefore, become the law of the

Lesson 1, Debate Instructions

Team Choctaw Chief Pushmataha (Response to Tecumseh), Continued

Choctaws and Chickasaws, and Pushmataha will see that the will of the majority, so recently expressed, is rightly carried out to the letter. If, after this decision, any Choctaw should be so foolish as to follow your imprudent advice and enlist to fight against the Americans, thereby abandoning his own people and turning against the decision of his own council, Pushmataha will see that proper punishment is meted out to him, which is death. You have made your choice; you have elected to fight with the British. The Americans have been our friends and we shall stand by them. We will furnish you safe conduct to the boundaries of this Nation, as properly befits the dignity of your office. Farewell, Tecumseh. You will see Pushmataha no more until we meet on the fateful warpath.

Source: Deloria Jr., Vine and Junaluska, Arthur (Speakers). *Great American Indian Speeches, Vol. 1* (Phonographic Disc). New York: Caedmon, 1976. Available from the American Rhetoric Online Speech Bank, *http://www.americanrhetoric.com/speeches/nativeamericans/chiefpushmataha.htm*

Lesson 1, Debate Instructions
Team Tecumseh

Task: You are about to address a group of fellow Indians in the Indiana Territory. Many of these Indians are considering joining with you and your brother in your attempt to unify all Indians and to reclaim lands the Indians have lost to white settlers. You are determined to convince them that joining with the Prophet and yourself is the only choice for the future survival of the Indian people. You have great anger at the way the whites have abused the Indian people, divided them, and taken their land. You have worked and fought for years to unify the Indian people outside tribal lines against the white settlers. You have fought in wars and even lost your father in one of them. Your job is to convince the Indian people that they must stop selling the land and that ultimately everything will be gone and the traditional Indian way of life will be destroyed. Likewise, convince them that they have been cheated by white land agents and that they must unify to reclaim all the land that has been lost. Tell them that unless all Indian nations come together, they have no hope of stopping the tide of white settlement.

Although the letter is addressed to William Henry Harrison, governor of Indiana, you can still make the same arguments to your fellow Indians. Use both ideas and actual quotations from the passages presented here to make a persuasive speech that you will read aloud to the assembled Indians. The speech must be no fewer than 200 words, 100 of which must be in your own words and 100 of which should be in the form of direct quotes from the two passages. Write in the first person and in the present tense, making use of "I" statements. You may both take turns reading or select one reader. You may write more than 200 words if you wish.

Passage 1

Houses are built for you to hold councils in; the Indians hold theirs in the open air. I am a Shawnee. My forefathers were warriors. Their son is a warrior. From them I only take my existence. From my tribe I take nothing. I have made myself what I am. And I would that I could make the red people as great as the conceptions of my own mind, when I think of the Great Spirit that rules over us all. . . . I would not then come to Governor Harrison to ask him to tear up the treaty. But I would say to him, "Brother, you have the liberty to return to your own country." You wish to prevent the Indians from doing as we wish them, to unite and let them consider their lands as

Lesson 1, Debate Instructions

Team Tecumseh, Continued

the common property of the whole. You take the tribes aside and advise them not to come into this measure. . . . You want by your distinctions of Indian tribes, in allotting to each a particular, to make them war with each other. You never see an Indian endeavor to make the white people do this. You are continually driving the red people, when at last you will drive them into the great lake, where they can neither stand nor work. Since my residence at Tippecanoe, we have endeavored to level distinctions, to destroy village chiefs, by whom all mischiefs were done. It is they who sell the land to the Americans. Brother, this land that was sold, and the goods that were given for it, was only done by a few. . . . In the future we are prepared to punish those who propose to sell land to the Americans. If you continue to purchase them, it will make war among the different tribes, and at last I do not know what will be the consequences among the white people. The way, the only way to stop this evil, is for the red men to unite in claiming a common and equal right in the land, as it was at first, and should be now—for it was never divided, but belongs to us all. No tribe has the right to sell, even to each other, much less to strangers. . . . Sell a country! Why not sell the air, the great sea, as well as the earth? Did not the Great Spirit make them all for the use of his children? How can we have confidence in the white people? When Jesus Christ came upon the earth you killed him and nailed him to the cross. You thought he was dead, and you were mistaken. You have the Shakers among you, and you laugh and make light of their worship. Everything I have told you is the truth. The Great Spirit has inspired me.

Source: Bryan, William Jennings. *The World's Famous Orations.* New York: Funk and Wagnalls, 1906. Available from *http://www.bartleby.com/268/8/4.html*

Passage 2

These lands are ours. No one has a right to remove us, because we were the first owners. The Great Spirit above has appointed this place for us, on which to light our fires, and here we will remain.

Source: Dictionary of Canadian Biography. Available from *http://www.biographi.ca/EN/ShowBio.asp?BioId= 36806&query=tecumseh*

LESSON 2
Recreating the Battle of Tippecanoe

DEFINING MOMENT II

MATERIALS NEEDED

EXCERPTS FROM WILLIAM HENRY HARRISON

- Observation 1, p. 140
- Observation 2, p. 140
- Observation 3, p. 141
- Observation 4, p. 141
- Observation 5, p. 142
- Observation 6, p. 142
- Observation 7, p. 143

EXCERPTS FROM SOLDIERS

- Observation 1, p. 144
- Observation 2, p. 144
- Observation 3, p. 145
- Observation 4, p. 145
- Observation 5, p. 146
- Observation 6, p. 146
- Observation 7, p. 147

EXCERPT FROM INDIAN

- Observation 1, p. 147

MAP

- Battle of Tippecanoe, p. 148

On November 18, 1811, General William Henry Harrison wrote an official dispatch to the secretary of war about the Battle of Tippecanoe. In this battle, Indian troops led by the Prophet, attacked 1,100 U.S. soldiers and militia that Harrison had led against them. Harrison had taken advantage of the fact that Tecumseh was away then recruiting new warriors and making alliances with other tribes. Harrison had hoped to draw the Prophet into battle, defeat him, and disperse the main center of operations for Tecumseh and the Prophet at Prophetstown. At 4:00 a.m. the Indians attacked the well-prepared and well-defended U.S. camp. The battle lasted for two hours, and the Indians were put to flight. The U.S. army moved onto the nearby village of Prophetstown, found it deserted, and burned it to the ground.

In this lesson, students will gain insight into and practice in the art of recreating a historical battle using only written narratives. By reading various firsthand accounts of the Battle of Tippecanoe, students will envision the lay of the land, the different attack points, the troop positions, and the ultimate outcomes of the theater of war. Students will draw their own bird's-eye view maps and compare them to a published battlefield map.

To begin, the teacher should tell the class that they will use firsthand accounts of the Battle of Tippecanoe to figure out what really happened. The teacher should distribute all of the excerpts (one for each pair of students). The goal for each pair is to contribute small pieces of information and insight that they find in their document to help create a bird's-eye view map of the battlefield and troop positions. Each student group should read their excerpt and create a large map of what they think is happening based on their excerpt. Then, the teacher should have the class compile their findings to recreate the battlefield, and together students should identify troop movements, attacks, or positions. Finally, the teacher should distribute the actual battlefield map and lead a discussion with the students, comparing and contrasting their work with the published map.

LESSON 3
The British Enter the Conflict

MATERIALS NEEDED

DOCUMENT

- Indian Account of the Battle of Tippecanoe, p. 149

POLITICAL CARTOON

- A Scene on the Frontiers, p. 150

HANDOUT

- Dialogue for A Scene on the Frontiers, p. 125

During the years after the American Revolution, a rocky relationship existed between the United States and Britain. Although both countries shared a common heritage and advantageous trading arrangements, there was still conflict between the two nations both at sea and on the border between Canada and the United States. In the region of the Great Lakes and what was called at the time the Northwest Territory, the British maintained a reasonably strong military presence, including control and occupation of forts that were technically on American soil. Likewise, the British were providing some amount of weapons to various Indian tribes and encouraging them to cause trouble for the white settlers moving west. At sea, the British Navy began harassing American merchant ships and sailors to such an extent that many citizens began clamoring for war. War did break out in 1812 between the two countries and Tecumseh allied himself and his remaining braves to the British cause. He died in a battle in Canada on the Thames River near Moravian Town. Ironically, the attacking U.S. general was William Henry Harrison, the same general who had defeated Tecumseh's brother the Prophet at the Battle of Tippecanoe.

In this lesson students will investigate Great Britain's role in widening the Indian war, by dissecting written and visual evidence related to English participation. As part of the lesson, students will redesign an anti-British political cartoon.

The first document students will analyze is an account of the Battle of Tippecanoe written by an Indian in which he describes the British role in that battle. It is important to note that this battle took place before the War of 1812 began. The second primary source is a political cartoon that appeared in an American newspaper during the War of 1812. The content is deliberately inflammatory and depicts an Indian warrior scalping a fallen U.S. soldier and receiving weapons in return. The arrangement between the British and their Indian allies was probably never as overt as the cartoon suggests, but there is strong evidence that the British were supplying the Indians with guns and ammunition.

Continues on next page

DEFINING MOMENT II

Lesson 3

The British Enter the Conflict, Continued

The teacher should distribute the document Indian Account of the Battle of Tippecanoe and divide the students into groups of three to read and answer the following questions in writing:

- What is the writer's impression of the Prophet?
- What positive things does the writer say about the Prophet? What negative things does he say?
- According to the author, what role did the British (the white men who came from Canada) play in this battle?
- Why do you think they dressed like Indians?
- Why was there a conflict over when the attack should begin?
- Do you think this is an accurate or reliable source? Why? Why not?
- Do you think the British played a role in this battle? Why? Why not?

After students have analyzed evidence that the English might have been involved in instigating the Indians to war, the teacher should distribute the political cartoon, A Scene on the Frontiers, and have the students answer the following questions in writing:

- What do you think the purpose of this cartoon and poem were?
- Do you think it was made by an American or an English cartoonist? Why?
- What do the captions "secret service mone," and "G.R." tell the viewer?
- How is the British general depicted?
- How are the Indians depicted?

Finally, the teacher should distribute the handout Dialogue for A Scene on the Frontiers, and students will act out a living tableau. In their groups of three, each student will write one line of dialogue that relates to the image. The dialogue should show that the students are aware of the basic message of the cartoonist but they can also add some humor. Once the students have written their lines, they will stand in front of the class in the same position as the figures for whom they are speaking. Ideally, the image could be projected in the background on a screen.

Lesson 3, Handout
Dialogue for A Scene on the Frontiers

▲ Cartoonist denounces British and Indian depredations on the American frontier during the War of 1812, alluding specifically to the practice of offering bounties for American scalps. The cartoon may have been prompted by the August 1812 massacre at Chicago and the purchase of American scalps there by British Colonel Henry Proctor. (Library of Congress)

LESSON 4
The Image of War

MATERIALS NEEDED

IMAGE

- Colonel Johnson's Engagement with the Savages, p. 151

The image Colonel Johnson's Engagement with the Savages depicts the Battle of the Thames (Moravian Town) and gives a numbered description of various events taking place during the battle. The battle began as an attack by U.S. soldiers against a combined British and Indian defense, but when the British lines broke, they retreated or surrendered. Tecumseh's forces, who had been positioned on the flank to hit the U.S. soldiers with crossfire, found themselves alone. The battleground soon turned to woods and swampland and many U.S. mounted soldiers had to dismount and fight hand-to-hand with Tecumseh's men. U.S. cavalry officer Colonel Richard Mentor Johnson led the attack in the woods and is said to have personally killed Tecumseh.

In this lesson, students will participate in a detailed analysis of the image and will evaluate the bias within. The teacher should distribute the image Colonel Johnson's Engagement with the Savages and ask students to analyze the image and read the captions. The teacher should then lead a class discussion, using the following questions as a guide:

- Do you think this image was designed by an Indian or a white American? Why?

- How are the U.S. soldiers depicted? How are the Indians depicted?

- Which group (U.S. soldiers or Indians) seems to be presented as the more noble?

Next, the students will design their own battlefield cartoon depicting this same event. They may use simple drawings or stick figures if they are not artistically inclined. In their cartoon they should try to create some of the same events and make numbered captions, but from the viewpoint that the Indians might have had.

LESSON 5
Tecumseh's End and Death Song

MATERIALS NEEDED

DOCUMENTS

- Letter from Tecumseh to British General Henry Proctor, pp. 152–153

- Excerpt from Tecumseh's Death Song, p. 154

After many years of trying to organize the Indian people into a unified resistance against the increasing white settlement of the Old Northwest Territory, Tecumseh ended by making common cause with British Canadian soldiers in the War of 1812. Although much of the momentum for an all-Indian alliance had withered away after his brother's loss at the Battle of Tippecanoe, Tecumseh was determined to continue his goal of removing white settlers from his land. After control of Lake Erie fell to American naval commander Oliver Hazard Perry, Tecumseh was forced to make one last stand alongside British general Proctor at the Battle of the Thames in Canada. Tecumseh died in the fighting, and General Henry Proctor fled the field.

In the letter written by Tecumseh to General Proctor just before the British-Indian loss to William Henry Harrison at the Battle of the Thames, Tecumseh, frustrated that General Proctor was continuing to retreat in the face of an advancing General Harrison, chastises Proctor. Tecumseh, who died at the Battle of the Thames in Canada in 1813, was by all accounts a remarkable man. A gifted speaker, leader, orator, and organizer of men, he was nevertheless unable to realize his goal of a pan-Indian state and the reclamation of lost Indian land. As part of his legacy he left behind his often quoted Death Song. Tecumseh's life seemed to represent conflict between a peaceful vision of a well-spent Indian life and frustration over external forces he could not fully control. These two forces are seen perhaps no more clearly than in these two selections of his writing.

The purpose of this lesson is to humanize Tecumseh, while revealing his frustration with the British allies. This is a creative summary project that will require students to pull together all that they have learned and experienced in the previous lessons. Students will create a "found poem" based on a letter and song written by Tecumseh before his death. A found poem is one in which students select already written words, phrases, lines, and so on and reorganize them into a new structure.

First, the teacher should provide students with a copy of the documents Letter from Tecumseh to British General Henry Proctor and Excerpt from Tecumseh's Death Song. The teacher should instruct the students to read both aloud in class or quietly to themselves. Students will then create their own 20-line found poem. They should alternate between the two selections choosing statements that have strong impact. They may also repeat lines. Next, students should assemble into groups of four and share their poems with each other. Each group should then vote on the best poem and present it to the whole class. The class can conclude by selecting the best poem.

Tecumseh and the Westward Movement

Lesson 1, Image
Tecumseh

TECUMSEH.

◄ Tecumseh was a well-known Shawnee military leader in the early 19th century. Image created/published between 1860 and 1900. (Library of Congress)

DEFINING MOMENT II

Lesson 1, Image
The Prophet

▲ A Shawnee mystic and the brother of Tecumseh, Tenskwatawa was the first of two influential Indians to be called the Prophet, appointing himself prophet in 1805. Laulewasika was his given name, but he adopted the name Elkswatawa, and later Tenskwatawa, the Shawnee Prophet. (McKenney, Thomas L. and James Hall. *The Indian Tribes of North America*, 1836–1844)

Lesson 1, Image
Indiana Territorial Governor William Henry Harrison

◀ William Henry Harrison, governor of the Indiana Territory and later president of the United States. Painting by James R. Lambdin. (Library of Congress)

Lesson 1, Document

Passage Written by Tecumseh to William Henry Harrison, 1810

Houses are built for you to hold councils in; the Indians hold theirs in the open air. I am a Shawnee. My forefathers were warriors. Their son is a warrior. From them I only take my existence. From my tribe I take nothing. I have made myself what I am. And I would that I could make the red people as great as the conceptions of my own mind, when I think of the Great Spirit that rules over us all. . . . I would not then come to Governor Harrison to ask him to tear up the treaty. But I would say to him, "Brother, you have the liberty to return to your own country." You wish to prevent the Indians from doing as we wish them, to unite and let them consider their lands as the common property of the whole. You take the tribes aside and advise them not to come into this measure. . . . You want by your distinctions of Indian tribes, in allotting to each a particular, to make them war with each other. You never see an Indian endeavor to make the white people do this. You are continually driving the red people, when at last you will drive them into the great lake, where they can neither stand nor work. Since my residence at Tippecanoe, we have endeavored to level distinctions, to destroy village chiefs, by whom all mischiefs were done. It is they who sell the land to the Americans. Brother, this land that was sold, and the goods that were given for it, was only done by a few. . . . In the future we are prepared to punish those who propose to sell land to the Americans. If you continue to purchase them, it will make war among the different tribes, and at last I do not know what will be the consequences among the white people. The way, the only way to stop this evil, is for the red men to unite in claiming a common and equal right in the land, as it was at first, and should be now—for it was never divided, but belongs to us all. No tribe has the right to sell, even to each other, much less to strangers. . . . Sell a country! Why not sell the air, the great sea, as well as the earth? Did not the Great Spirit make them all for the use of his children? How can we have confidence in the white people? When Jesus Christ came upon the earth you killed him and nailed him to the cross. You thought he was dead, and you were mistaken. You have the Shakers among you, and you laugh and make light of their worship. Everything I have told you is the truth. The Great Spirit has inspired me.

Source: Bryan, William Jennings. *The World's Famous Orations.* New York: Funk and Wagnalls, 1906. Available from *http://www.bartleby.com/268/8/4.html*

Lesson 1, Document

Passage Written by the Prophet to William Henry Harrison, 1808

Father, It is three years since I first began with that system of religion which I now practice. The white people and some of the Indians were against me; but I had no other intention but to introduce among the Indians, those good principles of religion which the white people profess. I was spoken badly of by the white people, who reproached me with misleading the Indians; but I defy them to say that I did anything amiss. Father, I was told that you intended to hang me. When I heard this, I intended to remember it, and tell my father, when I went to see him, and relate to him the truth. I heard, when I settled on the Wabash, that my father, the governor, had declared that all the land between Vincennes and fort Wayne, was the property of the Seventeen Fires. I also heard that you wanted to know, my father, whether I was God or man; and that you said if I was the former, I should not steal horses. I heard this from Mr. Wells, but I believed it originated with himself. The Great Spirit told me to tell the Indians that he had made them, and made the world—that he had placed them on it to do good, not evil. I told all the red skins, that the way they were in was not good, and that they ought to abandon it. That we ought to consider ourselves as one man; but we ought to live agreeably to our several customs, the red people after their mode, and the white people after theirs; particularly, that they should not drink whiskey; that it was not made for them, but the white people, who alone knew how to use it; and that it is the cause of all the mischief which the Indians suffer; and that they must always follow the directions of the Great Spirit, and we must listen to him, as it was he that made us: determine to listen to nothing that is bad: do not take up the tomahawk, should it be offered by the British, or by the long knives: do not meddle with any thing that does not belong to you, but mind your own business, and cultivate the ground, that your women and your children may have enough to live on. I now inform you, that it is our intention to live in peace with our father and his people forever. My father, I have informed you what we mean to do, and I call the Great Spirit to witness the truth of my declaration. The religion which I have established for the last three years, has been attended to by the different tribes of Indians in this part of the world. Those Indians were once different people; they are now but one: they are all determined to practice what I have communicated to them, that has come immediately from the Great Spirit through me. Brother, I speak to you as a warrior. You are one. But let us lay aside this character, and attend to the care of our children, that they may live in comfort and peace. We desire that you will join us for the preservation of both red and white people. Formerly, when we lived in ignorance, we were foolish; but now, since we listen to the voice of the Great Spirit, we are happy. I have listened to what you have said to us. You have promised to assist us: I now request you, in behalf of all the red people, to use your exertions to prevent the sale of liquor to us. We are all well pleased to hear you say that you will endeavor to promote our happiness. We give you every assurance that we will follow the dictates of the Great Spirit. We are all well pleased with the attention that you have showed us; also with the good intentions of our father, the President. If you give us a few articles, such as needles, flints, hoes, powder, &c., we will take the animals that afford us meat, with powder and ball.

Source: Drake, Benjamin. *Life of Tecumseh, and His Brother the Prophet With a Historical Sketch of the Shawanoe Indians.* Available from Project Gutenberg, *http://www.gutenberg.org/ebooks/15581*

DEFINING MOMENT II

Lesson 1, Document

Passages Written by William Henry Harrison

Notwithstanding the improper language which you have used towards me, I will endeavor to open your eyes to your true interests. Notwithstanding what white, bad men have told you, I am not your personal enemy. You ought to know this from the manner in which I received and treated you, on your visit to this place. Although I must say that you are an enemy to the Seventeen Fires [the 17 U.S. states], and that you have used the greatest exertions to lead them [the Indians] astray. In this you have been in some measure successful; as I am told they are ready to raise the tomahawk against their father. Yet their father, notwithstanding his anger at their folly, is full of goodness and is always ready to receive into his arms those of his children who are willing to repent, acknowledge their fault, and ask for his forgiveness. There is yet but little harm done which may be easily repaired. The chain of friendship which united the whites and the Indians, may be renewed and be as strong as ever. A great deal of that works depends on you—the destiny of those who are under your direction, depends upon the choice you make of the two roads which are before you. The one is large, open and pleasant and leads to peace, security and happiness; the other, on the contrary, is narrow and crooked and leads to misery and ruin. Don't deceive yourselves; do not believe that all nations of Indians united are able to resist the force of the Seventeen Fires. I know your warriors are brave, but ours are not less so. But what can a few brave warriors do against the innumerable warriors of the Seventeen Fires? Our blue-coats are more numerous than you can count. Our hunters are like the leaves of the forest or the grains of sand on the Wabash. Do not think that the red-coats can protect you; they are not able to protect themselves. They do not think of going to war with us. If they did, you would in a few moons see our flag wave over all the forts of Canada. What reason have you to complain of the Seventeen Fires? Have they taken anything from you? Have they ever violated the treaties made with the red men? You say they have purchased lands from those who had no right to sell them. Show that this is true and the land will be instantly restored. Show us the rightful owners of those lands which have been purchased—let them present themselves. The ears of your father will be opened to your complaints and if the lands have been purchased of those that did not own them, they will be restored to the rightful owners. I have full power to arrange this business; but if you would rather carry your complaints before your great father, the President, you shall be indulged. I will immediately take means to send you with those chiefs which you may choose to the city where your father lives. Everything necessary shall be prepared for your journey, and means taken for your safe return.

The mind of a savage is so constructed that he cannot be at rest, he cannot be happy unless it is acted upon by some strong stimulus. That which is produced by war is the only one that is sufficiently powerful to fill up the intervals of the chase. If he hunts in the winter he must go to war in the summer, and you may rest assured Sir, that the establishment of tranquility between the neighboring tribes will always be a sure indication of war against us.

Source: Drake, Benjamin. *Life of Tecumseh, and His Brother the Prophet With a Historical Sketch of the Shawanoe Indians.* Available from Project Gutenberg, *http://www.gutenberg.org/ebooks/15581*

Lesson 1, Document

Passage about Tecumseh by William Henry Harrison

The implicit obedience and respect which the followers of Tecumseh pay to him, is really astonishing, and more than any other circumstance bespeaks him one of those uncommon geniuses which spring up occasionally to produce revolutions, and overturn the established order of things. If it were not for the vicinity of the United States, he would, perhaps, be the founder of an empire that would rival in glory Mexico or Peru. No difficulties deter him. For four years he has been in constant motion. You see him to-day on the Wabash, and in a short time hear of him on the shores of lake Erie or Michigan, or on the banks of the Mississippi; and wherever he goes he makes an impression favorable to his purposes. He is now upon the last round to put a finishing stroke to his work. I hope, however, before his return that that part of the fabric which he considered complete will be demolished, and even its foundations rooted up. Although the greater part of his followers are attached to him from principle and affection, there are many others who follow him through fear; and he was scarcely a mile from town, before they indulged in the most virulent invectives against him. The Prophet is impudent and audacious, but is deficient in judgment, talents and firmness.

Source: Drake, Benjamin. *Life of Tecumseh, and His Brother the Prophet With a Historical Sketch of the Shawanoe Indians.* Available from Project Gutenberg, *http://www.gutenberg.org/ebooks/15581*

DEFINING MOMENT II

Lesson 1, Document

Passage about the Prophet by Thomas Jefferson

The Wabash Prophet is more rogue than fool, if to be a rogue is not the greatest of all follies. He arose to notice while I was in the administration, and became, of course, a proper subject for me. The inquiry was made with diligence. His declared object was the reformation of red brethren, and their return to their pristine manners of living. He pretended to be in constant communication with the Good Spirit; that he was instructed by Him to make known to the Indians that they were created distinct from the whites, of different natures, for different purposes, and placed under different circumstances adapted to their nature and destinies; that they must return from all the ways of the whites to the habits and opinions of their forefathers; that they must not eat the flesh of hogs, of bullocks, of sheep, etc., the deer and the buffalo having been created for their food; they must not make bread of wheat, but of Indian corn; they must not wear linen nor woolen, but must dress like their fathers, in the skins and furs of animals; they must not drink, and I do not know whether he extended his inhibition to the use of the gun and gunpowder, in favor of the bow and arrow. I concluded from all this that he was a visionary, enveloped in their antiquities, and vainly endeavoring to lead back his brethren to the fancied beatitudes of their golden age. I thought there was little danger of his making many proselytes from the habits and comforts they had learned from the whites, to the hardships and privations of savageism [sic], and no great harm if he did. But his followers increased until the British thought him worth corrupting and found him corruptible. I suppose his views were then changed; but his proceedings in consequence of them were after I left the administration, and are, therefore, unknown to me; nor have I been informed what were the particular acts on his part which produced an actual commencement of hostilities on ours. I have no doubt, however, that the subsequent proceedings are but a chapter apart, like that of Henry and Lord Liverpool in the book of the Kings of England.

Source: Drake, Benjamin. *Life of Tecumseh, and His Brother the Prophet With a Historical Sketch of the Shawanoe Indians.* Available from Project Gutenberg, *http://www.gutenberg.org/ebooks/15581*

Lesson 1, Document

Passage about William Henry Harrison by Isaac Rand Jackson

In person, General Harrison is tall and slender; his features are irregular, but bold and strongly marked; his eyes are dark, keen and penetrating; his forehead is high and expansive; his mouth peculiarly denotes firmness and genius; and the expression of his countenance is highly indicative of intelligence and benevolence of character. From early manhood he has never had the appearance of possessing a robust constitution; but from the activity and temperate habits of his past life, few men at his age, enjoy their moral and physical energies in such remarkable vigour. His manners are plain, frank and unassuming; and his disposition is cheerful, kind and generous, almost to a fault. In his private intercourse, he is beloved and esteemed by all who know him. In the various civil and military offices he has held, he has always been moderate and forbearing, yet firm and true to his trust. No other commander has ever been more popular with our militia, and the true secret cannot be better explained than by his own reply, when asked how he had gained this influence: "By treating them," said he, "with affection and kindness; by always recollecting that they were my fellow-citizens, whose feelings I was bound to respect; and by sharing with them, on every occasion, the hardships which they were obliged to undergo." His suavity of manners, his generosity and kindness of heart, invariably won him the warm affections of those who were placed under his authority, while his moderation, his disinterestedness, his scrupulous attention to the public interests, and the wisdom with which he exercised the extensive powers intrusted to him, commanded the respect and confidence of his fellow-citizens. General Harrison is likewise strictly and truly a pious man. Though he has always been noted for his particular attention to public worship and Christian offices, yet religion with him has not been a Sabbath-day garment only, but rather an everyday familiar habit— not a mere sense of incumbent duty, but a warm and spontaneous feeling, kindled into life in his early youth, and forming the hope and firm reliance of his manhood and declining years. The writer of a biographical notice of him, declares that he deems it no betrayal of confidence to say, that he has more than once, on entering at daybreak the chamber of General Harrison, found him on his knees at his bedside, absorbed in his devotions to his Maker, when he could not have supposed that any eye save that of his God was resting on him.

Source: Jackson, Isaac Rand. *The Life of Major-General William Henry Harrison*. Philadelphia: Grigg & Elliot, 1840 (pp. 89–90).

Lesson 1, Historical Background
The Shawnee Brothers: Tecumseh and the Prophet

Tecumseh was the best known and most admired opponent of white frontier expansion. He combined military skill and oratory brilliance to fashion one of the biggest pan-Indian alliances. He was also unique among his contemporaries in that he discouraged the traditional slaughter or torture of captives. Tecumseh's inspired leadership was alien to the usual norms of Native American leadership, however, and many older chiefs, feeling their authority threatened, refused to join his confederation. When Tecumseh died, his dream of a unified Native American state perished with him. Tecumseh (which means "Shooting Star") was born into the Crouching Panther Clan of the Shawnee Nation around 1768 in present-day Ohio. The frontier was in a perpetual state of unrest, as colonial Americans were flooding over the Appalachian Mountains and into traditional Native American hunting grounds. Friction between the two groups resulted in a war in 1774, in which Tecumseh's father was killed. Thereafter, Tecumseh expressed an undying hatred for whites, and after turning 16 years old, he joined numerous raiding parties. The successful conclusion of the American Revolution only increased the tempo of westward migration, and other wars resulted. In 1790 and 1791, Tecumseh gained renown as a scout and warrior and distinguished himself in the defeats of American military leaders Josiah Harmar and Arthur St. Clair. Three years later, he was present when Indian forces were defeated by Anthony Wayne at the Battle of Fallen Timbers.

With a small group of followers, Tecumseh left Ohio for the relative safety of the Indiana Territory, where they hoped to be far removed from further dealings with whites. After a decade of relative peace, Tecumseh's calm was shattered by a new series of land acquisitions. In 1804, the territorial governor of Indiana, William Henry Harrison, managed to convince several older chiefs to cede several million acres to the United States through treaties. Enraged by the prospect of losing additional hunting ground, Tecumseh established himself as a forceful opponent of further land sales. He went from tribe to tribe, arguing that because the land in question belonged to all Native Americans, none of it could be sold without the consent of all. His argument was backed by the teachings of his brother, Tenskwatawa (the Prophet), who invoked Native American religion to counteract the destructive effects of white culture. The unique combination of intertribal diplomacy and mystic revivalism promoted a surprising degree of unity among the tribes of the region, and they began resisting white overtures. Harrison parleyed unsuccessfully with Tecumseh in 1809 but was impressed by Tecumseh's intelligence, bearing, and resolve. He described the chief to Secretary of War William Eustis as "one of those uncommon geniuses, which spring up occasionally to produce revolutions and overturn the established order of things."

Tecumseh, wishing to expand his idea of confederation, next traveled as far west as Iowa and as far south as Florida to recruit new members. In Mississippi, the noted Choctaw chief Pushmataha rebuffed his stance with equal eloquence, but the Creek Nation of Alabama, then in the throes of its own religious revival, listened closely and began preparing for war against the whites. Tenskwatawa, or the Prophet, was an important Native

Lesson 1, Historical Background

The Shawnee Brothers, Tecumseh and the Prophet, Continued

American religious and political leader in the early days of the 19th century. He preached a message of returning to traditional ways and rejecting European goods and behavior. His better-known brother, Tecumseh, used the Prophet's message to try to build a pan-Indian confederation that would stop the expansion of the United States and its settlers. Tenskwatawa was born sometime in 1775 in what later became Ohio. He was awkward and unable to do many things because he had accidentally gouged his right eye out with an arrow when he was a boy. His parents favored his brother, Tecumseh, and largely ignored Tenskwatawa. He was unpopular among the Shawnee and often complained about his fate. He was an unsuccessful hunter and warrior and became an alcoholic. Tenskwatawa joined a war party led by Tecumseh that fought at the Battle of Fallen Timbers and apparently attended the negotiations and celebrations that surrounded the Treaty of Greenville in 1795. After the treaty was signed, Tenskwatawa lived with a small band of Shawnees led by Tecumseh, who lived in various locations in western Ohio and eastern Indiana.

While living at this location, Tenskwatawa experienced the first of several visions. He had unsuccessfully attempted to establish himself as a healer and a shaman, but in April 1805 he had a mystic experience in which he was given a view of Heaven and Hell. His spiritual guides told him that the Creator of Life had made the Indians, but that the Great Serpent, a source of evil, had created the white men. If the Indians did not turn away from the white man's ways and things, they would end in Hell. The "spawn of the Serpent" were aided in their attempts to corrupt the Native Americans by Indian witches who had adopted the cultural values of the white Americans. Tenskwatawa called for the Indians to limit their contacts with Americans. He allowed them to use firearms for personal defense but believed they must hunt with traditional weapons. European and American foods, clothing, manufactured goods, and especially alcohol were forbidden. Intertribal warfare was to be eliminated. In this way, the Indians would be revitalized. To mark his new role, he adopted the name of Tenskwatawa (which means "Open Door"), because his teachings were intended to provide a path to happiness and salvation for the Indians. White settlers had continued to encroach on Indian territory, and Native Americans were pushed out of their traditional lands. The game animals on which the Indians depended were wiped out. Epidemics swept through the villages. Many tribal communities disintegrated under the stress of alcohol, the corruption of traditional ways of living, and unchecked violence by the settlers. Many Indians looked for causes and solutions to their problems in the spiritual world. Tenskwatawa fit into a pattern of Indian mystics who preached revitalization and rebirth of the Indian way of life by returning to old ways and rejecting white products and ideas. Tenskwatawa's ideas spread rapidly among the Indians, especially after he successfully predicted an eclipse of the sun in June 1806. Many Indians visited his camp in 1807, causing great concern among the white American settlers and authorities. In 1808, Tecumseh and Tenskwatawa moved their followers to a new village at the junction of the Tippecanoe and Wabash rivers in western Indiana. They named the settlement Prophetstown.

Lesson 2, Excerpts from William Henry Harrison
Observation 1

A piece of dry oak land, rising about ten feet above the level of a marshy prairie in front toward the Prophet's town and nearly twice that high above a similar prairie in the rear, through which and near to this bank ran a small stream, clothed with willows and other brushwood. Towards the left flank this bench of land widened considerably but became gradually narrower in the opposite direction and at a distance of one hundred and fifty yards from the right flank terminated in an abrupt point.

Source: Tunnell, Harry D. *To Compel with Armed Force: A Staff Ride Handbook for the Battle of Tippecanoe.* Available from the Combined Arms Research Library, *http://www-cgsc.army.mil/carl/resources/csi/tunnell/tunnell.asp*

Lesson 2, Excerpts from William Henry Harrison
Observation 2

I had risen at a quarter after four o'clock, and the signal for calling out the men would have been given in two minutes, when the attack commenced. It began on the left flank; but a single gun was fired by the sentinels, or by the guard in that direction, which made not the least resistance, but abandoned their officer and fled into camp; and the first notice which the troops of that flank had of the danger, was from the yells of the savages a short distance from the line; but, even under these circumstances, the men were not wanting to themselves or to the occasion. Such of them as were awake, or were easily awakened, seized their arms and took their stations; others, which were more tardy, had to contend with the enemy in the doors of their tents.

Source: Frost, John. *The Presidents of the United States from Washington to Cleveland, Comprising Their Personal and Political History.* Boston: Lee and Shepard, 1889. Available from *http://libsysdigi.library.uiuc.edu/oca/Books2007–09/presidentsofunit00fros/*

Lesson 2, Excerpts from William Henry Harrison
Observation 3

The storm first fell upon Captain Barton's company, of the Fourth United States Regiment, and Captain Guiger's company of mounted riflemen, which formed the left angle of the rear line. The fire upon these was excessively severe, and they suffered considerably before relief could be brought to them. Some few Indians passed into the encampment near the angle, and one or two penetrated to some distance before they were killed. I believe all the other companies were under arms, and tolerably formed, before they were fired on.

Source: Frost, John. *The Presidents of the United States from Washington to Cleveland, Comprising Their Personal and Political History.* Boston: Lee and Shepard, 1889. Available from *http://libsysdigi.library.uiuc.edu/oca/Books2007–09/ presidentsofunit00fros/*

Lesson 2, Excerpts from William Henry Harrison
Observation 4

The morning was dark and cloudy. Our fires afforded a partial light, which, if it gave us some opportunity of taking our position, was still more advantageous to the enemy, affording them the means of taking a surer aim. They were, therefore, extinguished as soon as possible. Under these discouraging circumstances, the troops (nineteen-twentieths of whom had never been in an action before) behaved in a manner that can never be too much applauded. They took their places without noise, and with less confusion than could have been expected from veterans placed in a similar situation. As soon as I could mount my horse, I rode to the angle that was attacked. I found that Barton's company had suffered severely, and the left of Guiger's entirely broken. I immediately ordered Cook's company, and the late Captain Wentworth's, under Lieutenant Peters, to be brought up from the center of the rear line, where the ground was much more defensible, and formed across the angle, in support of Barton's and Guiger's.

Source: Beard, Reed. *The Battle of Tippecanoe.* Tippecanoe Pub., 1889. Available from *http://www.rootsweb.com/~ usgenweb/ky/tippecanoe/chapter5.html*

Lesson 2, Excerpts from William Henry Harrison
Observation 5

My attention was then engaged by a heavy firing upon the left of the front line, where were stationed the small company of United States riflemen (then, however, armed with muskets), and the companies of Baen, Snelling and Prescott, of the Forth Regiment. I found Major Daveiss forming the dragoons in the rear of those companies, and understanding that the heaviest part of the enemy's fire proceeded from some trees about fifteen or twenty paces in front of those companies, I directed the major to dislodge them with a part of the dragoons. Unfortunately, the major's gallantry determined him to execute the order with a smaller force than was sufficient, which enabled the enemy to avoid him in the front and attack his flanks. The major was mortally wounded, and his party driven back. The Indians were, however, immediately and gallantly dislodged from their advantageous position, by Captain Snelling, at the head of his company.

Source: Beard, Reed. *The Battle of Tippecanoe.* Tippecanoe Pub., 1889. Available from *http://www.rootsweb.com/ ~usgenweb/ky/tippecanoe/chapter5.html*

Lesson 2, Excerpts from William Henry Harrison
Observation 6

In the course of a few minutes after the commencement of the attack, the fire extended along the left flank, the whole of the front, the right flank and part of the rear line. Upon Spencer's mounted riflemen, and the right of Warrick's company, which was posted on the right of the rear line, it was excessively severe. Captain Spencer, and his first and second lieutenants, were killed, and Captain Warrick mortally wounded. Those companies, however, still bravely maintained their posts; but Spencer's having suffered so severely, and having originally too much ground to occupy, I reinforced them with Robb's company of riflemen, which had been driven, or, by mistake, ordered from their position in the left flank, toward the center of the camp, and filled the vacancy that had been occupied by Robb with Prescott's company of the Fourth United States Regiment. My great object was to keep the lines entire—to prevent the enemy from breaking into the camp, until daylight should enable me to make a general and effectual charge.

Source: Beard, Reed. *The Battle of Tippecanoe.* Tippecanoe Pub., 1889. Available from *http://www.rootsweb.com/ ~usgenweb/ky/tippecanoe/chapter5.html*

Lesson 2, Excerpts from William Henry Harrison
Observation 7

With this view I had reinforced every part of the line that had suffered much; and as soon as the approach of morning discovered itself, I withdrew from the front line Snelling's, Posey's (under Lieutenant Allbright) and Scott's, and from the rear line Wilson's companies, and drew them up upon the left flank; and, at the same time, I ordered Cook's and Baen's companies—the former from the rear, and the latter from the front line—to reinforce the right flank, forseeing [sic] that, at these points, the enemy would make their last efforts. Major Wells, who commanded on the left flank, not knowing my intentions precisely, had taken the command of these companies—had charged the enemy before I had formed the body of dragoons with which I meant to support the infantry; a small detachment of these were, however, ready, and proved amply sufficient, for the purpose. The Indians were driven by the infantry at the point of the bayonet, and the dragoons pursued and forced them into a marsh, where they could not be followed. Captain Cook and Lieutenant Larrabee had, agreeably to my order, marched their companies to the right flank and formed them under fire of the enemy; and, being then joined by the riflemen of that flank, had charged the Indians, killed a number, and put the rest to precipitate flight.

Source: Beard, Reed. *The Battle of Tippecanoe.* Tippecanoe Pub., 1889. Available from *http://www.rootsweb.com/~usgenweb/ky/tippecanoe/chapter5.html*

DEFINING MOMENT II

Lesson 2, Excerpts from Soldier
Observation 1

The orderly was standing by preparing to give the signal for stand-to. General Harrison was in his tent talking to some of his officers. Meanwhile, Lieutenant Colonel Bartholomew, the field officer of the day, was inspecting his sentries. Some soldiers were awake or waking up in preparation for stand-to. Other soldiers were adding fuel to the warming fires as a drizzling rain fell. Then, the sentry near Major Wells' command fired at an infiltrating Indian. The wounded Indian cried out, and his companions rushed the camp from several sides, pursuing the retreating sentries. As the sentries retired into the camp, the units on the perimeter were awake and forming for battle.

Source: Tunnell, Harry D. *To Compel with Armed Force: A Staff Ride Handbook for the Battle of Tippecanoe.* Available from the Combined Arms Research Library, *http://www-cgsc.army.mil/carl/resources/csi/tunnell/tunnell.asp*

Lesson 2, Excerpts from Soldier
Observation 2

It was my constant custom to assemble all of the field officers at my tent every evening by signal to give them the watch word and their instructions for the night—those given for the night of the 6th were that each Corps which formed a part of the exterior line of the encampment should hold its own ground until relieved. The Dragoons were directed to parade dismounted in case of night attack with their pistols in their belts and to act as a Corps de Reserve. The Camp was defended by two Captains Guards consisting of four noncommissioned officers and 42 privates and two Subaltern Guards of twenty noncommissioned officers and privates. The whole under the command of the field officer of the day. The troops were regularly called up an hour before day and made to continue under arms until it was quite light.

Source: Tunnell, Harry D. *To Compel with Armed Force: A Staff Ride Handbook for the Battle of Tippecanoe.* Available from the Combined Arms Research Library, *http://www-cgsc.army.mil/carl/resources/csi/tunnell/tunnell.asp*

DEFINING MOMENT II

Lesson 2, Excerpts from Soldier
Observation 3

At or near 4 o'clock in the morning I was alarmed by the discharge of a gun, on which I immediately repaired to my company, where I found my men all paraded at their posts. The position of the men during the night, together with myself, while at rest was lying on our arms with our clothes on—as for myself I lay with my boots on greatcoat on & accouterments buckled round me, with my rifle in my arms. At the report of the gun I had no more to do than to throw off my blanket, put my hat on & go to my company which was eight or ten steps from my tent, the time might be one or two minutes, where I found my men as above mentioned.

Source: Tunnell, Harry D. *To Compel with Armed Force: A Staff Ride Handbook for the Battle of Tippecanoe.* Available from the Combined Arms Research Library, *http://www-cgsc.army.mil/carl/resources/csi/tunnell/tunnell.asp*

Lesson 2, Excerpts from Soldier
Observation 4

I awoke about four o'clock the next morning. . . . A drizzling rain was falling and all things were still and quiet throughout the camp. I was engaged in making a calculation when I should arrive at home. In a few moments I heard the crack of a rifle. . . . I had just time to think that some sentinel was alarmed and had fired his rifle without a real cause, when I heard the crack of another rifle, followed by an awful Indian yell all around the encampment. In less than a minute I saw the Indians charging our line most furiously and shooting a great many balls into our camp fires, throwing the live coals into the air three or four feet high. The sentinels, closely pursued by the Indians, came to the line of the encampment in haste and confusion. My brother, William Naylor, was on guard. He was pursued so rapidly and furiously that he ran to the nearest point on the left flank, where he remained with a company of regular soldiers until the battle was near its termination. A young man, whose name was Daniel Pettit, was pursued so closely and furiously by an Indian as he was running from the guard fire to our lines, that to save his life he cocked his rifle as he ran and turning suddenly round, placed the muzzle of his gun against the body of the Indian and shot an ounce ball through him. The Indian fired his gun at the same instant, but it being longer than Pettit's the muzzle passed by him and set fire to a handkerchief which he had tied round his head.

Source: Tunnell, Harry D. *To Compel with Armed Force: A Staff Ride Handbook for the Battle of Tippecanoe.* Available from the Combined Arms Research Library, *http://www-cgsc.army.mil/carl/resources/csi/tunnell/tunnell.asp*

Lesson 2, Excerpts from Soldier
Observation 5

The men that were to crawl upon their bellies into the camp were seen in the grass by a white man who had eyes like an owl, and he fired and hit his mark. The Indian was not brave. He cried out. He should have lain still and died. Then the other men fired. The other Indians were fools. They jumped out of the grass and yelled. They believed what had been told them, that a white man would run at a noise made in the night. Then many Indians who had crept very close so as to be ready to take scalps when the white men ran, all yelled like wolves, wild cats and screech owls; but it did not make the white men run. They jumped up right from their sleep with guns in their hands and sent a shower of bullets at every spot where they heard a noise. They could not see us. We could see them, for they had fires. Whether we were ready or not we had to fight now for the battle was begun.

Source: Tunnell, Harry D. *To Compel with Armed Force: A Staff Ride Handbook for the Battle of Tippecanoe.* Available from the Combined Arms Research Library, *http://www-cgsc.army.mil/carl/resources/csi/tunnell/tunnell.asp*

Lesson 2, Excerpts from Soldier
Observation 6

At this moment my friend Wamock was shot by a rifle ball through his body. He ran few yards and fell dead on the ground. Our lines were broken and a few Indians were found on the inside of the encampment. In a few moments they were all killed. Our lines closed up and our men in the proper places. One Indian was killed in the back part of Captain Geiger's tent, while he was attempting to tomahawk the Captain. The Indians made four or five most fierce charges on our lines, yelling and screaming as they advanced, shooting balls and arrows into our ranks. At each charge they were driven off in confusion, carrying their dead and wounded as they retreated

Source: Tunnell, Harry D. *To Compel with Armed Force: A Staff Ride Handbook for the Battle of Tippecanoe.* Available from the Combined Arms Research Library, *http://www-cgsc.army.mil/carl/resources/csi/tunnell/tunnell.asp*

Lesson 2, Excerpts from Soldier
Observation 7

I rode to the angle that was attacked. I found that Barton's company had suffered severely and the left of Geiger's entirely broken. I immediately ordered Cook's and the late Capt. Wentworth's under Lieut. Peters to be brought up from the centre of the rear line where the ground was much more defensible and formed across the angle in support of Barton's and Geiger's.

Source: Tunnell, Harry D. *To Compel with Armed Force: A Staff Ride Handbook for the Battle of Tippecanoe.* Available from the Combined Arms Research Library, *http://www-cgsc.army.mil/carl/resources/csi/tunnell/tunnell.asp*

Lesson 2, Excerpts from Indian
Observation 1

As soon as daylight came our warriors saw that the Prophet's grand plan had failed—that the great white chief was alive riding fearlessly among his troops in spite of bullets, and their hearts melted. After that the Indians fought to save themselves, not to crush the whites. It was a terrible defeat. Our men all scattered and tried to get away. The white horsemen chased them and cut them down with long knives swords.

Source: Tunnell, Harry D. *To Compel with Armed Force: A Staff Ride Handbook for the Battle of Tippecanoe.* Available from the Combined Arms Research Library, *http://www-cgsc.army.mil/carl/resources/csi/tunnell/tunnell.asp*

Lesson 2, Map
Battle of Tippecanoe

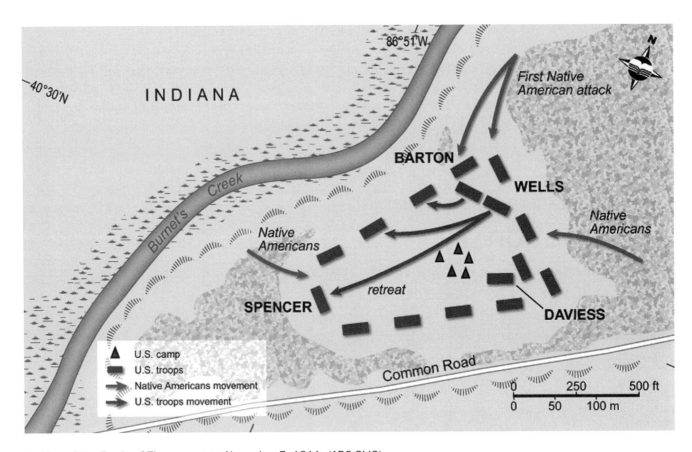

▲ Map of the Battle of Tippecanoe on November 7, 1811. (ABC-CLIO)

Lesson 3, Document

Indian Account of the Battle of Tippecanoe

He [Tecumseh] was not at the battle of Tippecanoe. If he had been there it would not have been fought. It was too soon. It frustrated all of his plans. He [The Prophet] was a great medicine. He talked much to the Indians and told them what had happened. He told much truth, but some things that he told did not come to pass. He was called "The Prophet." Your people new [knew] him only by that name. He was very cunning, but he was not so great a warrior as his brother, and he could not control the young warriors so well who were determined to fight. Perhaps your people do not know that the battle of Tippecanoe was the work of white men who came from Canada and urged us to make war. Two of them who wore red coats were at the Prophet's Town the day that your army came. It was they who urged Elskatawwa [the Prophet] to fight. They dressed themselves like Indians, to show us how to fight. They did not know our mode. We wanted to attack at midnight. They wanted to wait till daylight.

Source: Tunnell, Harry D. *To Compel with Armed Force: A Staff Ride Handbook for the Battle of Tippecanoe.* Available from the Combined Arms Research Library, *http://www-cgsc.army.mil/carl/resources/csi/tunnell/tunnell.asp*

Lesson 3, Political Cartoon
A Scene on the Frontiers

▲ Cartoonist denounces British and Indian depredations on the American frontier during the War of 1812, alluding specifically to the practice of offering bounties for American scalps. The cartoon may have been prompted by the August 1812 massacre at Chicago and the purchase of American scalps there by British Colonel Proctor. *Note:* The text in the original image has been edited to make it more readable by students. (Library of Congress)

Lesson 4, Image

Colonel Johnson's Engagement with the Savages

A View of Col. Johnson's Engagement with the Savages (Commanded by Tecumseh) near the Moravian Town, October 5, 1812.

1. Col. Johnson heroically defending himself against the attack of an Indian Chief.
2. The American Infantry firing upon a body of the enemy on the left.
3. A dismounted Dragoon personally engaged with one of the enemy.
4. The cavalry pursuing the retreating savages across the hills.
5. Tecumseh is rallying his men, and encouraging to return to the attack.
6. A savage is in the act of scalping a wounded drummer of the American Infantry.
7. The savages pursued by the cavalry, retreating to a swamp on the left.
8. The enemy (rallied by their commander Tecumseh) returning to the attack.

▲ A View of Colonel Richard Mentor Johnson's Engagement with the "Savages" (Commanded by Tecumseh) near Moravian Town on October 5, 1813. *Note:* The text in the original image has been edited to make it more readable by students. (Library of Congress)

Lesson 5, Document

Letter from Tecumseh to British General Henry Proctor

Father, listen to your children! You have them now all before you. The war before this, our British father gave the hatchet to his red children, when old chiefs were alive. They are now dead. In that war our father took them by the hand without our knowledge, and we are afraid that our father will do so again at this time. Summer before last, when I came forward with my red brethren and was ready to take up the hatchet in favor of our British father, we were told not to be in a hurry, that he had not yet determined to fight the Americans.

Listen! When war was declared, our father stood up and gave us the tomahawk and told us that he was ready to strike the Americans; that he wanted our assistance; and that he would certainly get us our lands back, which the Americans had taken from us.

Listen! You told us, at that time, to bring forward our families to this place, and we did so—and you promised to take care of them, and that they should want for nothing, while the men would go and fight the enemy; that we need not trouble ourselves about the enemy's garrisons; that we knew nothing about them; and that our father would attend to that part of the business. You also told your red children that you would take good care of your garrison here, which made our hearts glad.

Listen! When we were last at the Rapids, it is true we gave you little assistance. It is hard to fight people who live like groundhogs. Father, listen! Our fleet has gone out; we know they have fought; we have heard the great guns, but know nothing of what has happened to our father with one arm. Our ships have gone one way, and we are much astonished to see our father tying up everything and preparing to run away the other, without letting his red children know what his intentions are. You always told us to remain here and take care of our lands. It made our hearts glad to hear that was your wish.

Lesson 5, Document

Letter from Tecumseh to British General Proctor, Continued

Our great father, the King, is the head, and you represent him. You always told us that you would never draw your foot off British ground; but now, Father, we see you are drawing back, and we are sorry to see our father doing so without seeing the enemy. We must compare our father's conduct to a fat animal that carries its tail upon its back, but when affrighted, it drops it between its legs and runs off.

Listen, Father! The Americans have not yet defeated us by land; neither are we sure that they have done so by water—we therefore wish to remain here and fight our enemy, should they make their appearance. If they defeat us, we will then retreat with our father. At the battle of the Rapids, last war, the Americans certainly defeated us, and when we retreated to our father's fort in that place, the gates were shut against us. We were afraid that it would now be the case, but instead of that, we now see our British father preparing to march out of his garrison.

Father! You have got the arms and ammunition which our great father sent for his red children. If you have an idea of going away, give them to us, and you may go and welcome, for us. Our lives are in the hands of the Great Spirit. We are determined to defend our lands, and if it is His will, we wish to leave our bones upon them.

Source: Howe, Henry. *Historical Collections of the Great West, Vol. I.* Cincinnati: Howe, 1857 (pp. 230–231).

DEFINING MOMENT II

Lesson 5, Document

Excerpt from Tecumseh's Death Song

So live your life that the fear of death can never enter your heart. Trouble no one about their religion; respect others in their view, and Demand that they respect yours. Love your life, perfect your life, Beautify all things in your life. Seek to make your life long and Its purpose in the service of your people.

Prepare a noble death song for the day when you go over the great divide. Always give a word or a sign of salute when meeting or passing a friend, Even a stranger, when in a lonely place. Show respect to all people and Bow to none. When you arise in the morning, give thanks for the food and For the joy of living. If you see no reason for giving thanks, The fault lies only in yourself. Abuse no one and nothing, For abuse turns the wise ones to fools and robs the spirit of its vision.

When it comes your time to die, be not like those whose hearts Are filled with fear of death, so that when their time comes They weep and pray for a little more time to live their lives over again In a different way. Sing your death song and die like a hero going home.

Source: Bent, Devin. "Tecumseh: A Brief Biography." Available from The James Madison Center, *http://www.jmu. edu/madison/center/main_pages/madison_archives/era/native/tecu@VSH*:mseh/bio.htm

Tecumseh and the Westward Movement

Glossary Terms

assimilation and allotment era

The assimilation and allotment era refers to the period from 1871 to the end of the 1920s in which the United States sold or gave land to non-Indians in the hope of forcing the Native Americans to assimilate into white American society. In 1871, the U.S. government removed sovereign nation status from individual tribes but did not give U.S. citizenship to Native Americans. To solve this problem, the 1887 Dawes Act stated that individual Indians who received allotted parcels of land would become citizens. It was not until the 1924 Snyder Act that all Native Americans became citizens.

breastworks

Breastworks are barricades usually about chest-high that shield defenders from enemy fire. Usually made of earth, defenders would kneel behind them when being fired upon and stand to shoot. When firearms needed to be reloaded, breastworks also provided protection during the relatively lengthy process.

Indiana Territory

Created in 1800, the Indiana Territory was originally part of the Old Northwest Territory and at its greatest extent covered the present-day states of Indiana, Illinois, Wisconsin, Michigan, and parts of Minnesota. Its first governor was William Henry Harrison, who was also superintendent of Indian Affairs, served until 1812. During his tenure as governor, he signed several treaties with Native American nations to cede their land to the United States.

removal era

The removal era refers to the period beginning with the passage of the May 30, 1830, Removal Act and ending in the mid-1850s. The Removal Act sought to move, by force if necessary, Native Americans residing in the eastern United States into what was considered "Indian Country," or present-day Oklahoma. This would be most visible in 1833 when President Andrew Jackson ordered the Cherokees from their land in Georgia and initiated what would become known as the Trail of Tears.

scalping

Scalping was the process of removing the skin of the scalp with the hair still attached. To Native Americans, this process and the kill that it signified had profound religious connotations as both a corporeal and spiritual victory over an opponent. It was highly ritualized, and scalps would often be decorated and used in ceremonies. To Europeans, on the other hand, it was merely evidence of Indian brutality. Scalp bounties were created by colonial governments to reward individuals who returned from combat with the scalps of their opponents.

DEFINING MOMENT II

Biographies

William Eustis

William Eustis was born in Cambridge, Massachusetts, on June 10, 1753. He became a surgeon on the Patriot side of the American Revolutionary War and later served as senior camp surgeon. He also became an anti-Federalist. In March 1809, James Madison nominated Eustis to be secretary of war, despite the fact that Eustis had no military administrative experience. Obsessing over the details of administration rather than focusing on the big picture, he also quarreled often with generals. Eustis did make some improvements, though, such as new coastal fortifications. At the onset of the War of 1812, there was much confusion on the ground, no commanding general, and several generals did not know the boundaries of their command. When Eustis's mistakes became obvious to Congress, he submitted a letter of resignation. Eustis won election to the governorship of Massachusetts in 1823 and 1824, but he died of pneumonia on February 6, 1825.

William Henry Harrison

William Henry Harrison was born on February 9, 1773, at Berkley, Virginia. He was an active participant in many of the Indian Wars within the Old Northwest Territory, including the Battle of Fallen Timbers. Harrison served as the first governor of Indiana Territory from 1800 through 1812. As governor, he negotiated 10 land treaties with the Native Americans, purchasing millions of acres of land. Shawnee leaders Tecumseh and the Prophet chafed at the encroachment of white settlers, and Harrison tried in vain to keep the peace and ease tensions. During the Battle of Tippecanoe on November 7, 1811, Harrison's forces overwhelmed the Native Americans under the Prophet. Harrison would continue fighting during the War of 1812, eventually defeating British forces and Tecumseh at the Battle of the Thames. After the war, Harrison ran repeatedly for the House of Representatives and the Senate before winning the presidency and taking office on March 4, 1841. He died one month later on April 4, 1841.

Thomas Jefferson

Thomas Jefferson was born on April 13, 1743, at the Shadwell plantation in Virginia. At the start of the American Revolutionary War, Jefferson penned the Declaration of Independence. Ever afraid of a strong centralized government, Jefferson founded the Democratic-Republican Party to counter the aims of the Federalist Party, led by Alexander Hamilton, which advocated a loose interpretation of the Constitution. He was elected vice president in 1796 but became disenchanted when President John Adams instituted many of Hamilton's programs. Jefferson was elected to the presidency in 1800. Despite following a strict interpretation of the Constitution, when the Louisiana Territory became available Jefferson jumped at the offer. The territory had been the ancestral home of many Native American nations and the acquisition would lead to several Indian wars over the next few decades. After serving a second term as president, Jefferson retired to his Virginia mansion, Monticello. He died on July 4, 1826.

Richard Johnson

Richard Mentor Johnson was born on October 17, 1780, in what is now Louisville, Kentucky. He trained as a lawyer and was elected to the state legislature in 1804. Two years later, he won a seat in the U.S. House of Representatives as a Democrat. Johnson would soon ally himself with other war hawks like Henry Clay. When the War of 1812 broke out, Johnson commanded a regiment of mounted Kentucky riflemen. He fought at the Battle of the Thames, where he was severely wounded before allegedly killing the Shawnee chief Tecumseh. Johnson returned to Congress as a war hero. After losing his seat in 1819, he was elected to the U.S. Senate, only to go back to the House after losing his Senate seat. In 1836, Andrew Jackson, a close friend of Johnson's, picked him as the vice presidential candidate on the successful Democratic ticket with Martin Van Buren. Johnson served as vice president under Van Buren from 1837 to 1841. Johnson died on November 19, 1850.

Henry Procter

Henry Procter was born in Ireland, probably in 1763. In the final years of the American Revolutionary War, he bought a commission and by 1800 he was a lieutenant colonel of the 41st Regiment. With war again imminent, Procter organized the Canadian militia and established an alliance with the Shawnee leader Tecumseh. When Major General Isaac Brock died on October 13, 1812, Procter assumed command of the British Right Division, and in defending Upper Canada he relied heavily on his alliance with the Native Americans. Procter fought in several battles during the War of 1812. After a string of victories, his forces were defeated at the Battle of the Thames and his ally, Tecumseh, was killed. For this defeat, he was court-martialed and found guilty of poor judgment, which largely ended his career. He died in Bath, England, on October 13, 1822.

Pushmahata

Pushmahata was probably born in 1765 in the Six Towns District of the Choctaw Nation, the site of present-day Noxubee County, Mississippi. By 1804, he had risen to mingo, or the principle chief, of the Choctaws, having proven himself to be skilled in warfare, as an orator, and as a negotiator. Pushmahata realized early on that the

Continues on next page

whites were strong and must remain allies with the Choctaws. As such, when Tecumseh began gathering strength and touring to gather recruits, Pushmahata would travel behind him and give his own speech urging peace. Throughout the War of 1812 and the Creek War, the Choctaws remained allied to the United States. Pushmahata fought on the side of the Americans in the Creek War and became known as the "Indian general." Choctaw warriors would fight in the battles at Econochaca, Horseshoe Bend, and New Orleans. After the War of 1812, Pushmahata signed other cession treaties in 1816 and 1820 and invested a great deal of tribal wealth into establishing schools. He died on December 24, 1824.

Tecumseh

Tecumseh is believed to have been born around March 1768 in a Shawnee village along the Scioto River in Ohio. When the flow of westward migration increased after the American Revolutionary War ended in 1783, Tecumseh participated in several battles against the United States before fleeing west to the Indiana Territory. In the early 1800s, he and his brother, the Prophet, urged the Shawnees to return to traditional Indian values. After Indiana territorial governor William Henry Harrison forced the Native Americans in the region to sell vast tracts of land to the United States, Tecumseh lobbied for a pan-Indian movement to prevent further white expansion. When Tecumseh was away in 1811, the Prophet was soundly defeated at the Battle of Tippecanoe, dealing a serious blow to Tecumseh's goal of an Indian confederacy. Tecumseh fought on the side of the British during the War of 1812. He was killed at the Battle of the Thames on October 5, 1813. Tecumseh remains one of the best-known Native American leaders in history.

Tenskwatawa

Tenskwatawa, a younger brother of Tecumseh, was born with the name Lalawethika in early 1775. He was a troubled youth who became an alcoholic. In 1805, he fell into a coma, and when he awoke he claimed to have seen a vision in which he went to Heaven and spoke with the "Great Spirit." He then journeyed to Hell and saw what abandoning the old ways had wrought. Upon waking, he swore off alcohol and took the name Tenskwatawa, although he came to be known as "the Prophet." He went on a preaching tour to enlist men in Tecumseh's pan-Indian confederation, making his base at Prophetstown. On November 7, 1811, the Prophet led a night raid against Indiana territorial governor William Henry Harrison's forces, claiming his men would be immune to bullets. Harrison emerged victorious at the Battle of Tippecanoe and destroyed Prophetstown. The Prophet and Tecumseh had a falling out after the defeat. The Prophet died in Kansas in November 1836.

Groups and Organizations

Chickasaws

The Chickasaws were one of the so-called Five Civilized Tribes of the Southeast (in addition to the Cherokees, Choctaws, Creeks, and Seminoles). Sharing the Western Muskogean language family with the Choctaws, the Chickasaws settled primarily in present-day northern Mississippi. Based on their shifting fortunes in war and diplomacy, the Chickasaws also claimed territory extending into other states. During the colonial period, the Chickasaws were aggressively courted by the British, French, and Spanish as each colonial power vied for security and commerce in the region. After the late 1600s, the Spanish were barely a presence, and the Chickasaws gravitated toward the British. However, they fought against the British in Pontiac's Rebellion and with the British in the American Revolutionary War, the latter out of fear of American westward expansion. From the early 1800s until the 1820s, Chickasaws began migrating west, ceding land in several treaties, and then ceding all lands east of the Mississippi in 1832. About 3,000 were forcibly removed in the Indian Territory (present-day Oklahoma) after 1837.

Chippewas

The Chippewa tribe (also known as the Ojibwe, Ojibwas, Ojibways, or more properly as the Anishinabes) constituted the largest Native American nation of the upper Great Lakes region. Living in widely dispersed communities located in present-day Ontario and Manitoba, Canada, Michigan, Wisconsin, and Minnesota, the Chippewa population during the colonial period was estimated at about 35,000. Because of their geographical location, the Chippewas had little involvement in conflicts between colonial European powers in the 17th century. However, they did come into conflict with the Iroquois Confederation during the Beaver (Iroquois) Wars of 1641–1701 and were one of the few peoples to turn back the mighty Five Nations of the Iroquois Confederation. The Chippewas avoided the first three imperial wars between England and France. However, with the outbreak of the French and Indian War, the French convinced many Chippewas to join their cause. The Chippewas largely stayed out of the American Revolutionary War, and though they were interested in the movements of Blue Jacket and Little Turtle and of Tecumseh and the Prophet, few warriors joined in the fighting.

Choctaws

The Choctaws are a Native American group whose territory included east-central Mississippi as well as parts of Alabama. The Choctaws were one of the so-called Five Civilized Tribes of the American Southeast (along with the Chickasaws, Creeks, Seminoles, and Cherokees). The Choctaw Nation traditionally resisted developing

Continues on next page

dependency on Europeans. Many of the wars the Choctaws fought in concerned the Chickasaws or Creeks on the opposing side, but the French alliance was solidified after the Choctaws took retribution on the Natchez in the Natchez Revolt of 1729. Up until the end of the 18th century, Choctaws, and especially Chief Red Shoes, played the British, French, and Spanish against each other in order to have the most advantageous position. Beginning in 1801, the Choctaws were under enormous pressure to cede their land. The U.S. government promised them land in the west, in the Oklahoma Territory, but those promises were rarely kept. Under the Indian Removal Act of 1830, the Choctaws and other Southeast tribes were forced to leave their homelands and relocate west of the Mississippi.

Creeks

The Creek Indians were a loose Southern confederacy of approximately 60 townships in western Georgia and the eastern part of modern-day Alabama. Although the Creeks had remained largely neutral in the colonial wars, under their charismatic statesman, Alexander McGillivary, they fought on the British side in the American Revolution and resisted the western expansionist attempts of Georgia during 1785–1787. After 1796, the Upper Creek townships underwent a native religious revival and their warriors, known as Red Sticks, were greatly influenced by the Shawnee chief Tecumseh. The Creeks proved to be fierce opponents of U.S. forces during the War of 1812. After McGillivary's death, the Lower Creek townships came under the influence of Benjamin Hawkins, the federal agent to the Creeks, and began a policy of assimilation in the hope that this would preserve their lands. When Little Warrior began attacking southern frontier settlements, he was hunted down and murdered. This began a civil war between the White Sticks who wanted peace and the Red Sticks who fought on the side of the British.

Shawnees

The Algonquian-speaking Shawnee Nation consisted of five divisions: the Macquachakes, the Chillicothes, the Thawekilas, the Piquas, and the Kispokis. Heavy involvement in the fur trade beginning in the early 18th century soon left many Shawnees in the clutches of alcohol and debt. Most Shawnee bands were pro-French in the colonial wars, but some were steadfast British trade partners and military allies, especially those bands that came under the control of the Iroquois. Most Shawnees participated in Pontiac's Rebellion in 1763. After 1777, the Shawnees proved to be strong allies of the British. The Shawnees, particularly under Blue Jacket, continued to fight to defend against U.S. expansion and refused to be bound by the Treaty of Greenville in 1795. In the early 19th century, the brothers Tecumseh and the Prophet launched a pan-Indian movement to halt white expansion. The Prophet's defeat at the Battle of Tippecanoe and Tecumseh's death during the War of 1812 ended any hope of an Indian confederation.

Events

American Indian Wars

The American Indian Wars took place in the period between roughly 1500 and 1890 and can be divided into four periods. The first set of wars took place primarily between Native Americans and Spanish conquistadors and missionaries during the 16th and 17th centuries in what would become the southwestern United States. The second series of wars occurred in the 17th century along the eastern seaboard and across what would become the border between Canada and the United States. This set of wars, which included King Philip's War and the French and Indian War, were fought between Native Americans and various European colonists representing the interests of England, France, and the Netherlands. The third set of wars occurred in the early 19th century, as Anglo-American settlements intruded deeper into Florida and the interior of the Ohio and Mississippi valleys, and would include the Creek War and the Seminole Wars. The final battles of the American Indian Wars occurred in the late 19th century, primarily on the Great Plains and in the southwestern United States, and would include the Red River War and the Battle of Little Bighorn.

Battle of Fallen Timbers

When the American Revolutionary War came to a close, the Continental Army was disbanded, leaving the United States with virtually no military protection in the 1780s. When the U.S. government sought to remove the Miamis from their lands, rather than going peacefully they rallied under Chief Little Turtle. This band would win two early victories against American forces, first against Josiah Harmar and then against Arthur St. Clair, who had a much larger force. George Washington sent Revolutionary War hero Anthony Wayne to deal with the Miamis. Wayne drilled his men for two years, adequately equipped them for the upcoming campaign, and ventured forth, building forts along the way for lines of communication. Wayne arrived at Fallen Timbers in August 1794. Knowing that the Miamis fasted before battle, Wayne did not begin the fighting for three days, during which the Indians became hungry and discouraged. The ensuing battle resulted in a major U.S. victory, and the Miamis were unable to regroup.

Battle of the Thames

In 1813, during the War of 1812, the British-Indian alliance had repelled three separate advances, and William Henry Harrison was to lead an assault into Canada. Having lost the Battle of Lake Erie, Henry Procter saw his position as untenable. After a long delay, Procter managed to convince the Shawnee leader, Tecumseh, to withdraw to the lower Thames. Tecumseh led his warriors and their families east. But Harrison, with a strong force of mounted infantry, quickly closed the gap between them. When the British and Native Americans reached the Moravian Town area, they were exhausted, hungry, and dispirited, and Procter only had one 6-pounder cannon

Continues on next page

on the site. In the battle that followed, Tecumseh was killed, probably by Richard Johnson, while leading an onslaught. With only 235 men in his command, Procter marched back to Ancaster, Ontario, where he was court-martialed and found guilty of poor judgment. Meanwhile, the death of Tecumseh left the Indian confederation shattered.

Battle of Tippecanoe

The Battle of Tippecanoe, fought between U.S. forces and Native American warriors, occurred on the banks of the Wabash River near Prophetstown (near present-day Lafayette, Indiana) on November 7, 1811. At the time, Shawnee leader Tecumseh and his brother, the Prophet, were seeking to create a pan-Indian alliance to resist further encroachment by their white neighbors. In November 1811, Tecumseh was away from Prophetstown recruiting other Native Americans for his confederation, leaving the Prophet in charge. William Henry Harrison, the governor of the Indiana Territory, sought to destroy Prophetstown and marched forth with nearly 1,000 men. While they camped outside Prophetstown, the Prophet urged a night attack, claiming that the white men's bullets could not harm them. After two hours of fighting, the Indians were in retreat. Harrison found the next day that Prophetstown had been abandoned, and he ordered the town torched. This battle served to solidify the British–Native American alliance and is sometimes considered the beginning of the War of 1812.

Lord Dunmore's War

Lord Dunmore's War began with a series of raids and counterraids between frontierspeople and several Native American nations of the Ohio Valley. These nations resented the Proclamation of 1763 and the Treaty of Fort Stanwix and rejected the right of the Iroquois to cede their lands. When settlers claimed the ceded territory in Kentucky, Shawnees and Wyandots sought to turn back the encroachers. By 1771, there was a confederacy of the Delawares, Mingos, Miamis, Ottawas, and Illinois that raided the frontier. In 1774, Virginia governor John Murray, Fourth Earl of Dunmore, sent out 2,000 militiamen into Shawnee territory, but this only caused further bloodshed. Although Shawnee chief Cornstalk wished for peace, none would listen until after the Indian defeat at Point Pleasant. Cornstalk then negotiated for peace with the Virginians, with both sides promising some concessions, and it was ratified by Mingo, Shawnee, Delaware, Wyandot, Iroquois, and Ottawa chiefs in the fall of 1775.

Red Stick War (Creek War)

The Red Stick War was a civil war within the Creek Nation. When the War of 1812 seemed imminent, the Creeks fell into two factions: the White Stick Creeks, who favored peace and neutrality, and the Red Stick Creeks, who were inspired by Tecumseh's message of resistance. A battle occurred at Burnt Corn Creek in which a group of Red Sticks fended off a white attack back to Fort Mims. Red Eagle attacked the fort in retaliation for Burnt Corn Creek, and the Red Sticks killed most of the inhabitants. The attack caused a major outcry, and the American populace determined to crush the Creeks. On March 27, 1814, Andrew Jackson's 15,000-man force decimated a force of 2,500 Red Sticks at the Battle of Horseshoe Bend. As a result of this defeat, the Creeks signed the Treaty of Fort Jackson on August 1, 1814, ceding more than 20 million acres of land to the United States.

War of 1812

The War of 1812 produced a number of long-term effects within the fledgling United States and Canada. For the former, it encouraged territorial expansion and accelerated the professionalization of the armed forces, and for the latter it solidified a feeling of nationhood as Canadians repeatedly came together to blunt the American advances into their territory. When war broke out, Britain was fighting a war in Europe against Napoleon and could not fight in North America with its full force. As such, it relied more on Canadian militia and Native American alliances. Although in many respects it was a naval war, there were also several instances of land and riverine war. The Battle of Tippecanoe, in which William Henry Harrison destroyed Shawnee leaders Tecumseh and the Prophet's home base of Prophetstown, is sometimes considered the beginning of the War of 1812.

Integration into National History Day
Using ABC-CLIO Web Sites for Researching Native American Resistance
Additional Native American Resistance Topic Ideas

Integration into National History Day

History is the story of people. The stories of individuals are exciting to study but when working with the theme *The Individual in History* there needs to be a sharp distinction between writing a biography and engaging in historical research. As the theme implies, the research will not be about the life of the individual but about looking closely at an event within the individual's life as a catalyst for change. In the resource book, *Native American Resistance,* King Philip and Tecumseh, both individuals displaying deep convictions, set about accomplishing their goals in distinctive ways. The historical research is not about the life of King Philip or Tecumseh but rather it is a microscopic look at a specific time in their lives when the historical context and the individuals' actions converged to create a historic change.

National History Day (NHD) is an educational program engaging students in grades 6 through 12 in historical research. After selecting a topic related to the NHD annual theme, students conduct research into primary and secondary sources. They enter projects in competitions using one of five different presentation formats: paper, performance, exhibit, Web site, or documentary.

Research projects on Native American resistance could encourage a student to present a paper on the individuals who led the Taos Revolt in 1847. Another student might create a documentary examining the American Indian Movement of the 1960s. Other projects might include creating an exhibit or Web site displaying the collected images and written texts of the Carlisle Indian Schools and the Native Americans' resistance to assimilation or a historical performance of the Navajo's Round Up at the Bosque Del Apache.

National History Day invites students to determine the historical significance of their chosen topic. Projects related to uncivil disobedience can be approached using different research processes:

- Using primary and secondary documents to place the topic into historical perspectives

- Building a timeline of events leading to the conflict to illustrate the significance of the topic

- Presenting an analysis of the conflict by introducing the historical context and people involved to deepen historical understanding

Regardless of the topic or approach, students should ask questions of their research and the meaning of their topic in history.

- Who were the people involved?

- What were their motivations?

- Why did the incident occur at this time in history?

- What was gained and what price was paid?

- What was the legacy of the decision?

- What if the opposing choice had been made? How would that have affected our world today?